RUSSIAN WORLD WAR II VOCABULARY

A RUSSIAN-ENGLISH GLOSSARY OF SPECIAL TERMS, SOLDIERS' EXPRESSIONS AND SLANG

Isaak Kobylyanskiy
and
Stuart Britton

Helion & Company Ltd

Helion & Company Limited
26 Willow Road
Solihull
West MidlandsB91 1UE
England
Tel. 0121 705 3393
Fax 0121 711 4075
Email: info@helion.co.uk
Website: www.helion.co.uk
Twitter: @helionbooks
Visit our blog http://blog.helion.co.uk/

Published by Helion & Company 2011. This hardback edition 2013.

Designed and typeset by Farr out Publications, Wokingham, Berkshire
Cover designed by Farr out Publications, Wokingham, Berkshire
Printed by Lightning Source, Milton Keynes, Buckinghamshire

ISBN 978-1-909384-06-4

British Library Cataloguing-in-Publication Data.
A catalogue record for this book is available from the British Library.

For details of other military history titles published by Helion & Company
Limited contact the above address, or visit our website: http://www.helion.co.uk.

We always welcome receiving book proposals from prospective authors.

Contents

Authors' Note   4

1. Special Military and Battle-Related Terms   7
    Some Aviation Terms   11
2. Military Ranks   13
3. Fortifications   15
4. Routes, Roads, Railroads, etc.   17
5. Weapons   20
    Handheld Weapons   20
    Other Weapons   21
6. Ammunition   25
7. Uniforms   27
8. Rank Insignia   30
    Prior to 1943   30
    After 1943   30
9. Decorations   32
    Orders   32
    Medals   33
    Anniversary medals   34
    Pre-war civil defense badges   34
10. Food, Drinks, Tobacco, etc.   36
    Food   36
    Alcohol   37
    Tobacco etc.   38
11. Abbreviations   39
12. Wartime Terms, Sayings and Colloquial Expressions   44
    Some Soviet Political Propaganda Wartime Slogans and Clichés   50
    Several aphorisms and pithy expressions attributed to Field-Marshal A.V. Suvorov (repeatedly published in the Soviet wartime press)   51
13. Demotic Words and Phrases   53
    Demotic Words and Phrases Related to a Person's Features   53
    Other Demotic Words and Phrases   55
    Indecent and Vulgar Words, Phrases and Expressions   62
14. Exclamations, Imperatives, Emotional Calls, Phrases etc.   64
15. Frontline Slang, Phrases and Soldiers' Humor   67
    Some special phrases   71
    A few funny anecdotes and amusing soldiers' tales which were popular at the front   72
    Rhymed humorous and vulgar expressions and playful folk songs   75

Authors' Note

A number of military historians from the USA, UK, USSR (today, Russia) continue to show their serious interest in the Great Patriotic War of the USSR against fascist Germany 1941–1945 (also known in the West as the Eastern Front of WWII). Over the past two decades, American scholars have published dozens of books devoted to the study of the most important operations of the Red Army on the fronts of the Great Patriotic War. Also, starting in the early 1990s, a number of memoirs written by ordinary WWII combatants were published in the USA, UK, Canada and other former Allied countries. In Russia, in addition to the publication of similar memoirs, hundreds of transcripts of interviews with common Great Patriotic War veterans became popular owing to a few specialized websites.

Along with their honesty, the WWII veterans' reminiscences are full of idiomatic expressions, specialized terms and abbreviations peculiar to that war. Regardless of their language, the memoirs reproduce the wartime vocabulary of the authors' nationalities and reading them was a difficult task for uninformed readers. As a consequence, special dictionaries appeared in print (such as Colby's[1] or Elkin's[2] etc.) and later on Internet websites (such as "Deadeye Glossary"[3] etc.) Unlike most of the Allied countries, no war jargon/slang dictionary has been published in Russia. This glossary is intended to begin to fill that gap.

The authors' work on creating this Russian-English glossary actually turned into a two-stage process: forming a specialized dictionary and then translating these unusual mostly figurative words, terms and expressions into English. In 2007, the idea to create such a glossary was put forward by one of the authors and from that time both authors began to accumulate appropriate words and phrases. The first attempt to form a short Russian-English glossary of war slang was undertaken in 2009.[4]

Meanwhile the authors accumulated additional word stock for the future glossary while translating several Russian memoirs into English as well as discovering the war slang found in dozens of published interviews with Soviet Great Patriotic War veterans.

Our teamwork resulted in around 900 entries and over 1400 Russian words which are represented in the glossary. All the collected material has been grouped into 15 subject chapters (several of those have appropriate subsections). It should be also noticed that among a large number of entries with slang words and phrases, you can find in the glossary many words which are represented in common or specialized dictionaries, too. We did so because these words accompanied the war slang very often.

Let's consider the main characteristics of the glossary's material. There were several sources to the language in this glossary.

The upheaval of the 1917 October Revolution and following Civil War, and the fundamental changes wrought by the political and social reforms and campaigns in the 1920s-1930s affected the Russian vocabulary substantially: a lot of new abbreviations and compound words were brought into daily use. Another set of figurative expressions arose as a result of Stalin's terrible purges of the 1930s, when people created euphemisms to avoid saying words like *search, arrest* and *execution.* Such expressions came into general circulation and also contributed to Russian wartime slang.

During the Great Patriotic War, the overwhelming majority of the Red Army consisted of servicemen from rural households and families. It is important to remember that in the 1930s, Soviet mass media was only beginning to spread to the rural population of the USSR, while that population's terms and expressions had always been a very important factor in the evolution of the Russian vocabulary. As a result, the peasants' own vocabulary didn't expand due to newly appearing words and terms. Instead, their vocabulary preserved a lot of words and expressions that were completely forgotten in the cities. The former peasants brought their language into the frontline trenches, and you will find a few such words in the glossary.

Some words also appeared under the harsh conditions of the USSR far rear, where civilians struggled under conditions of hard labor and malnutrition. The American lend-lease program of assistance to the USSR was also reflected in both frontline and far rear vocabularies. Finally, several terms and expressions of the WWI period were revived in the Red Army during the WWII. You will also find several samples of Russian pre-revolutionary humor, jokes and anecdotes that still circulated in the ranks of the Red Army.

Starting in the late 1930s, Stalin began to refer to the great military leaders of the Russian Imperial past more and more often. As the Great Patriotic War began, he continued the trend, and the powerful Soviet propaganda machine (which always keenly listened to any word used by its "Master" and "Teacher") immediately created a series of appeals and slogans of a new kind. The names of Suvorov, Kutuzov, Ushakov and other heroes of former wars became very popular in the propaganda output. It reached the frontlines trenches through the central and unit newspapers as well as via military political workers. Therefore the glossary contains a separate subsection of Chapter 12 with samples of wartime slogans and clichés.

It should be also remembered that in 1943, Stalin decided to adopt selective aspects of the Imperial Russian Army and of the olden days. The system of military ranks was overhauled, dropping the system of revolutionary ranks. Troops received new uniforms with new insignias of rank (which were both similar to pre-revolutionary ones). Several new orders and medals, named after Suvorov, Kutuzov, Ushakov, Nakhimov, Alexander Nevsky and Bogdan Khmel'nitsky were instituted. All of these wartime changes are reflected in the glossary as well.

The authors began this glossary as a translators' aid, but now we believe it will also be of interest to scholars, both military historians and linguists who work with original Russian military sources, especially of the Second World War period. We also count on amateurs who are interested in reading the mentioned sources.

Since the number of active World War II veterans is now diminishing quite rapidly, such written evidence as preserved memoirs, diaries, letters, etc., are becoming increasingly important subjects of study. We hope this glossary will be a useful tool in such studies.

Readers' suggestions for additional entries are welcome.

Notes

1. Entries of the Glossary are arranged within most of its chapters and subsections in the Russian alphabetical order, as follows:

А Б В Г Д Е Ё Ж З И Й К Л М Н О П Р С Т У Ф Х Ц Ч Ш Щ Ъ Ы Ь Э Ю Я

2. The Glossary employs the U. S. Library of Congress system of transliteration.
3. Vowels of stressed syllables in transcribed Russian words are bold-faced.
4. A few archaic words brought to the front line by natives of the Russian countryside are marked as *obsolete*.
5. Certain war- and military-related terms/expressions inherited from the Russian troops vocabulary of the First World War times are marked as *WWI*.

Endnotes

1   Colby E. *Army Talk. A Familiar Dictionary of Soldier Speech,* 2nd Ed. (Princeton: Princeton University Press, 1943).

2   Elkin F. "The Soldier's Language", *American Journal of Sociology,* 51 (1946): 414-442.

3   *"Deadeye Glossary WWII Army Jargon."* Available at http://www.rememberthedeadeyes.com/ DeadeyeGlossary.html

4   Drabkin A. & Kobylyanskiy I. *Red Army Infantrymen Remember the Great Patriotic War: A Collection of Interviews with 16 Soviet WW-2 Veterans* (AuthorHouse, 2009).

1

Special Military and Battle-Related Terms

Армия (armiia) = Army

Атака (ataka) = an attack.

Батальон (batal'on) = a battalion.

Батарея (batareia) = a battery.

Битва (bitva) and **сражение** (srazhenie) = a battle, an engagement, a large-scale fight.

Блокада (blokada) = the isolation of an area, city or harbor by enemy forces.

Боевое крещение (boevoe kreshchenie) = baptism of fire, a soldier's first experience with actual combat conditions.

Боевое охранение (boevoe okhranenie) = an advanced group of soldiers intended to provide early warning of an enemy probe or advance. Literally **боевое охранение** means *combat security*.

Боевой опыт (boevoi opyt) = combat experience.

Боевые действия (boevye deistviia) = combat operations for a specific objective.

Бригада (brigada) = a brigade.

Взвод (vzvod) = a platoon.

Военспецы (voenspetsy) = a category of former officers and NCOs of the Russian Tsarist army, who during the Civil War (1918-1921) had come over to the Red Army side mainly as volunteers. Even so, they were treated in the Red Army with distrust, especially of political workers. During the 1920s-40s some former **военспецы** had carved out prominent military careers as high Red Army leaders (several became Marshals of Soviet Union). However, in 1937 Stalin began the mass purging of the Soviet military leadership. It started with the "Tukhachevsky's case" which resulted in the execution of Marshal of Soviet Union M. N. Tukhachevsky; then a great many of less popular others were persecuted. Literally **военспецы** means *military specialists*.

Note: in contrast with **военспецы,** the majority of former Tsarists officers and NCOs were members of the anti-Soviet White Guards and fought actively against the Red Army troops.

Воинская часть (voinskaia chast') or just **часть** = a military unit or just a unit. Literally **часть** means *a part, a share.*

Воинские звания (voinskie zvaniia) = military ranks.

Воинское подразделение (voinskoe podrazdelenie) or just **подразделение** = a military element or unit.

Войсковая группировка (voiskovaia gruppirovka) = a regular or temporary large formation of several standard military units and some special ones. Its large-scale operations were planned and controlled by its own headquarters. Literally **войсковая группировка** means *a force grouping.*

Вооружённые силы (vooruzhionnye sily) = armed forces.

Гарнизон (garnizon) = a garrison.

Генеральный Штаб Красной Армии (general'nyi shtab krasnoi armii) = the General Staff of the Red Army. It was the main office of the **Ставка** (see below) during the Great Patriotic War. The General Staff performed strategic planning and supervision of the **Фронт** formations (see below).

Головной (golovnoi) and **передовой** (peredovoi) = advanced, leading, vanguard.

Действующая Армия (deistvuiushchaia armiia) = the Operating Army.

Десант (desant) = a landing force; also used to describe tank-riders known as **десантники** (desantniki).

Дивизион (divizion) = an artillery battalion.

Дивизия (diviziia) = a division.

Залп (zalp) = a salvo, a volley.

Замыкающий (zamykaiushchii) = the tail-end of a marching column, rear guard.

Заряд (zariad) = a charge or load, as in an explosive or blasting charge or load; also a shot, shell, round, or cartridge.

Казарма (kazarma) = barracks.

Караул (karaul) = a small detachment or a group of soldiers appointed to sentry duty or to control access to a place around the clock.

Командный пункт (КП) (komandnyi punkt [KaPe]) = a command post (CP)

Корпус (korpus) = a corps.

Круговая оборона (krugovaia oborona) = an all-round defense.

Манёвр (maniovr) = a maneuver.

Маневрирование (manevrirovanie) = maneuvering.

Маскировка (maskirovka) = camouflage or camouflaging.

Маскировочная сеть (maskirovochnaia set') = a camouflage net.

Маскировочные средства (maskirovochnye sredstva) = camouflage means.

Наблюдательный пункт (НП) (nabliudatel'nyi punkt [eNPe]) = an observation post (OP).

Наводить (navodit') and **нацеливать** (natselivat') = to aim, to zero in, to direct at, to target, as with weapons.

Направление (napravlenie) = a Russian official wartime term for an area or zone where operations are taking place. Literally **направление** means a direction or axis of advance or defense.

Наступление (nastuplenie) = an offensive.

Оборона (oborona) = a defense.

Оборонительный рубеж (oboronitel'nyi rubezh) = a defensive line.

Обходной манёвр (obkhodnoi maniovr) and **охват** (okhvat) = an outflanking maneuver.

Огневая позиция (ognevaia pozitsiia) and its colloquial form **огневая** = a weapon emplacement – the position, platform, or the like, for a gun, a mortar or battery and its accessories.

Огневая точка (ognevaia tochka) = a weapons emplacement or firing point (machine guns, mortars, anti-tank and anti-personnel guns etc.)

Огневой взвод (ognevoi vzvod) = a gun platoon.

Огневой заслон (ognevoi zaslon) = a fire barrage.

Окружение (okruzhenie) = an encirclement.

Операция (operatsiia) = an operation.

Орудийный расчёт (orudiinyi raschiot) = a gun crew.

Отвлекающий манёвр (otvlekaiuschii maniovr) = a diversionary maneuver.

Отдача (otdacha) and **откат** (otkat) = a recoil.

Отделение (otdelenie) = a squad, a subdivision of a platoon, a detachment.

Отступление (otstuplenie) = a retreat.

Передний край (perednii krai) and its colloquial form **передовая** (peredovaia) = a forward line of a formation's or unit's position; the front line.

Пехота (pekhota) = the infantry.

Плацдарм (platsdarm) = a staging area where troops are deploying for a future offensive operation. May also be translated as bridgehead. (Also see **предмостное укрепление** below).

Полк (polk) = a regiment.

Потери (poteri) = casualties.

Предмостное укрепление (predmostnoe ukreplenie) = a bridgehead – an initial foothold across a river barrier with the potential to expand and strengthen into a **плацдарм** (see above).

Разведка (razvedka) = a reconnaissance.

Разведка боем (razvedka boem) = an offensive probe designed to discover or test the enemy's strength (or to obtain other information). It can be performed even by a small detachment, such as a platoon. **Разведка боем** is often translated as *reconnaissance in force*.

Рейд (reid) = a raid.

Рекогносцировка (rekognostsirovka) = a preliminary reconnoitering of an area where a military unit will take its new position (the rout of approach to the area is also a subject of the reconnoitering). As a rule, a group of a unit's senior officers accomplish the reconnoitering.

Рота (rota) = a company.

Рубеж атаки (rubezh ataki) = an assault position; a line of attack; a jumping-off line.

Ставка Верховного Главнокомандования (stavka verkhovnogo glavnokomandovaniya) or just **Ставка** (stavka) = *(WW I)* the extraordinary organ of the highest military administration that executed the strategic guidance the Soviet Armed Forces during the Great Patriotic War. Literally **Верховное Главнокомандование** means *the Supreme High Command.*

Ударная Армия (udarnaia armiia) = an Assault or Shock Army.

Участок фронта (uchastok fronta) = a sector of the front.

Фланг (flang) = a flank.

Фронт (front) [1] = front, a line or zone of battle.

Фронт [2] = Front, a Soviet large-scale operational combat formation (usually consisting of several armies plus several attached armor and artillery corps and other assets).

Штаб (shtab) = headquarters, HQ.

Штурм (shturm) = a direct and violent assault on a stronghold.

Штурмовой отряд (shturmovoi otriad) = an assault detachment.

Эскадра (eskadra) = a naval squadron (a subdivision of a naval fleet).

Эскадрон (eskadron) = a cavalry squadron, a detachment of about one hundred of horsemen.

Эшелон (eshelon) = an echelon. (For another meaning of **эшелон** see Chapter 4).

Эшелонирование обороны (eshelonirovanie oborony) = disposing defense in depth; carrying out an echeloned defense.

Some Aviation Terms

Авианалёт (avianaliot) = an air raid.

Бомбардировщик (bombardirovshchik) = a bomber.

Бомбёжка (bombiozhka) = the process of bombing (see **бомбить** below).

Бомбить (bombit') = to bomb, to drop bombs on.

Бреющий полёт (breiushchii poliot) = a hedgehopping flight – a flight performed very close to the ground. Mostly used in low-flying attacks. Literally **бреющий полёт** means *a shaving flight*.

Воздушный бой (vozdushnyi boii) = an aerial combat.

Воздушный таран (vozdushnyi taran) = an aerial combat technique designed to destroy or disable the enemy's aircraft by collision or by cutting some its elements with blades of one's own propeller. **Воздушный таран** was first performed by Russian military pilot Piotr Nesterov in 1914 during the WW I.

Звено (zveno) = an air force flight (a subdivision of an air force squadron [see **эскадрилья** below]).

Истребитель (istrebitel') = a fighter.

Пара (para) = an air force element of two planes. One of them is the leading plane, the other is the supporting one. The Russian **пара** has two meanings: *a couple* and *a pair*.

Пикировать (pikirovat') = to dive.

Планировать (planirovat') = to glide, to fly without engine power.

Свободная охота (svobodnaia okhota) = a special type of fighter and bomber operation, where the pilot chooses on his/her own the route, altitude, speed of the aircraft, and, mainly, the specific target of the operation. Literally **свободная охота** means *a free hunt*.

Штурмовик (shturmovik) = a ground-attack aircraft.

Штурмовка (shturmovka) = a low-flying attack by a ground-attack aircraft.

Эскадрилья (esksdril'ia) = an air force squadron (a subdivision of an air forces unit).

2

Military Ranks

Красноармеец (krasnoarmeets) = Red Army soldier. Also, **солдат** (soldat) – a soldier, and **рядовой** (riadovoi) – a private.

Ефрейтор (efreitor) = a corporal.

Младший сержант (mladshii serzhant) = a junior sergeant.

Сержант (serzhant) = a sergeant.

Старший сержант (starshii serzhant) = a senior sergeant.

Старшина (starshina) = a sergeant major.

Младший лейтенант (mladshii leitenant) = a junior lieutenant.

Лейтенант (leitenant) = a lieutenant.

Старший лейтенант (starshii Leitenant) = a senior lieutenant.

Капитан (kapitan) = a captain.

Майор (maior) = a major.

Подполковник (podpolkovnik) = a lieutenant colonel.

Полковник (polkovnik) = a colonel.

Генерал-майор (general-maior) = a major-general.

Генерал-лейтенант (general-lieutenant) = a lieutenant-general.

Генерал-полковник (general-polkovnik) = a colonel-general.

Генерал армии (general armii) = a General of the Army.

Маршал Советского Союза (marshal sovetskogo soiuza) = a Marshal of the Soviet Union.

Флот (flot) = Navy or Fleet

Краснофлотец (krasnoflotets) = a Red Fleet seaman.

Старший краснофлотец (starshii krasnoflotets) = a senior Red Fleet seaman or a Red Fleet leading seaman.

Старшина 2-й статьи (starshina vtoroi stat'i) = a petty officer.

Старшина 1-й статьи (starshina pervoi stat'i) = a petty officer first class.

Главный старшина (glavnyi starshina) = a chief petty officer.

Мичман (michman) = a warrant officer or a master chief petty officer.

Младший лейтенант (mladshii leitenant) = a junior lieutenant.

Лейтенант (leitenant) = a lieutenant.

Старший лейтенант (starshii leitenant) = a senior lieutenant.

Капитан-лейтенант (kapitan-leitenant) = a lieutenant-captain.

Капитан 3-го ранга (kapitan tret'ego ranga) = a 3rd class captain.

Капитан 2-го ранга (kapitan vtorogo ranga) = a 2nd class captain.

Капитан 1-го ранга (kapitan pervogo ranga) = a 1st class captain.

Контр-адмирал (kontr-admiral) = a rear-admiral.

Вице-адмирал (vitse-admiral) = a vice-admiral.

Адмирал (admiral) = an admiral.

Адмирал флота (admiral flota) = an Admiral of the Fleet.

3

Fortifications

Амбразура (ambrazura) = an embrasure.

Бруствер (brustver) = a parapet, a breastwork.

Бункер (bunker) = a bunker, an underground shelter.

ДЗОТ (dzot) – abbreviated **дерево-земляная огневая точка** (derevo-zemlianaia ognevaia tochka) = a small, low, defensive structure constructed of earth and logs; an earth-and-timber emplacement.

ДОТ (dot) = abbreviated **долговременная огневая точка** (dolgovremennaia ognevaia tochka) that means a low, strongly fortified defensive structure such as a minor fortress, a concrete bunker or a pillbox.

Землянка (zemlianka) = a dugout – a rough shelter formed by an excavation in the ground.

Крепость (krepost') = a fortress.

Минное заграждение (minnoe zagrazhdenie) = a minefield barrier.

Минное поле (minnoe pole) = a minefield – an area of land or sea in which explosive mines have been placed.

Накат (nakat) = a flat covering layer of logs over a dugout; sometimes there could be two or more similar layers, one over another.

Нейтральная полоса (neitral'naia polosa) = a no man's land. **Нейтралка** (neitralka) is a colloquial name for **нейтральная полоса.**

Окапываться (okapyvat'sia) = to entrench, to dig-in.

Окоп (okop) and **ячейка** (iacheika) = an entrenchment, a foxhole.

Переправа (pereprava) [1] = a structure that provides a passage over a river (such as a pontoon bridge, temporary bridge etc.)

Переправа [2] = an operation to get across a river.

Предполье (predpol'e) = a moderately fortified zone lying between the zone of main fortification and the no man's land.

Проволочное заграждение (provolochnoe zagrazhdenie) = a wire entanglement.

Противотанковый ёж (protivotankovyi iozh) = an anti-tank hedgehog – a three-dimensional anti-tank obstacle made of three beams of rolled steel.

Противотанковый ров (protivotankovyi rov) = an anti-tank ditch.

Пулемётное гнездо (pulemiotnoe gnezdo) = a well-established machine-gun emplacement. Literally **пулемётное гнездо** means *a machine-gun nest*.

Траншея (transheia) = a trench – a long, narrow excavation in the ground, the earth from which is thrown up in front to serve as a shelter from enemy fire or attack.

Укрепление (ukreplenie) [1] = a defensive structure consisting of walls or mounds built around a stronghold.

Укрепление [2] = the process of strengthening defensive positions with fortifications.

УР (ur) – abbreviated **укрепрайон** [ukrepraion] – a compound word for **укреплённый район** [ukreplionnyi raion] (which literally means *a fortified district*) = the name of a particular fortified zone and also given to the **УР** unit that initially is deployed there. In case of a retreat or a successful offensive the unit would fight as a special infantry unit subordinated to the Army or Front Command. Most of the **УР**s were built at a definite distance from the USSR's border in 1930s.

Эскарп (eskarp) = a steep inner slope or wall of an antitank ditch; an escarpment.

4
Routes, Roads, Railroads, etc.

Болото (boloto) and **топь** (top') = a swamp, a marsh.

Большак (bol'shak) and **грейдер** (greider) = colloquial terms for a built but unpaved (or macadam) road which is suitable for two-way traffic and is provided with ditches along both its sides.

Буерак (buerak), **балка** (balka), **долина** (dolina), **лощина** (loshchina), **овраг** (ovrag) = terms for a ravine, a gully.

Буксовать (buksovat') = to skid.

Булыжная мостовая (bulyzhnaia mostovaia) = a cobblestone road.

Гать (gat') = a log-path over a swamp; a corduroy road.

Грунтовая дорога (gruntovaia doroga), **просёлочная дорога** (prosiolochnaia doroga) and **просёлок** (prosiolok) = terms for a dirt road.

Двухколейный путь (dvukhkoleinyi put') = double track.

Железная дорога (zheleznaia doroga) = a railroad. Literally **жедезная дорога** could be translated as an iron road.

«Зелёная улица» (zelionaia ulitsa) – literally a green street = a Russian figurative expression that in the wartime years usually related to the Soviet railroad system. At that time it consisted of countless long single-track sections with rare short double-track sections. The railroad traffic controllers managed to accomplish an uninterrupted movement for hundreds of military **эшелон**s (see below) in such a difficult situation by establishing long stretches of one-way traffic. In other words, they gave these moving **эшелон**s a "green street" or non-stop conditions (as if a vehicle is moving along a street with all traffic lights being green).

In general terms, **«зелёная улица»** describes a movement or an action without standard or regular restrictions. So, for example, a corrupted official can give the "green street" to a criminal gang.

Косогор (kosogor) and **склон** (sklon) = terms for a slope.

Кювет (kiuvet) = an approximately one-yard-deep ditch next to a **большак** (see above) or asphalt road shoulder.

Напрямик (napriamik) = straight on, across country.

Насыпь (nasyp') = a railroad embankment.

Обочина (obochina) = a narrow strip of land next to a road; a road shoulder.

Однопутная жедезная дорога (odnoputnaia zheleznaia doroga) and its nickname **однопутка** (odnoputka) = a single-track railroad.

Пассажирский вагон (passazhirskii vagon) = a coach.

Платформа (platforma) = an open freight car with short boards.

Полустанок (polustanok) = a small railroad station; a way station.

Разъезд (raziezd) = a railway siding for shunting trains.

Рокада (rokada) = a road for switching troops from one point to another concealed from the enemy. **Рокада** is usually parallel to the front line at a distance of some several miles.

Семафор (semafor) = a semaphore.

Сопка (sopka), **курган** (kurgan) and **холм** (kholm) = terms for a small hill.

Состав (sostav) = a train. **Состав** could be also translated as *a composition, a structure, a staff.*

Стрелка (strelka) = a movable section of railroad track used in transferring a train from one set of tracks to another; a railroad switch.

Стрелочник (strelochnik) = a railroad worker who controls the **стрелка** (see above). His/her position is the lowest among other railroad workers. This fact underlay a very popular Russian saying: **Стрелочник всегда виноват** (strelochnik vsegda vinovat) which means that the **стрелочник** is always a culprit of any bad event or situation (even if it is obvious that the actual culprit is some VIP). In other words, whoever else was guilty, the blame would be laid on his/her lowest subordinate.

Теплушка (teplushka) = a freight car reequipped as a railroad carriage for about twenty-odd soldiers.

Товарный вагон = a freight car.

Гропа (tropa) and **тропинка** (tropinka) = terms for a path and for a small path respectively.

Тягач (tiagach) = a powerful caterpillar tractor designed for towing heavy military weapons, such as tanks, self-propelled guns, trucks etc.

Увязнуть в болоте (uviaznut' v bolote) = to get stuck in a swamp.

Узкоколейная железная дорога (uzkokoleinaia zheleznaia doroga) and its nickname **узкоколейка** (uzkokoleika) = a narrow gauge railroad.

Урочище (urochishche) = a certain zone which essentially differs from the surrounding area; for example, a marsh in the heart of a forestland, or a wooded ravine in an otherwise barren flatland, or a patch of woods in a cleared area. In old Russia any **урочище** had been given a proper name (often after a neighboring settlement; for example: **Урочище** Ivanovka).

Шпала (shpala) = a railroad tie.

Шоссе (shosse) = a long two-way road paved with asphalt.

Эшелон (eshelon) = a military train (see another meaning of **эшелон** in Chapter 1).

5

Weapons

Handheld Weapons

Автомат (avtomat) = an informal colloquial name for any submachine gun.

«Вальтер» (val'ter) = the German Walther P 38 – 9mm pistol, produced as the standard service pistol for the Wehrmacht.

Карабин (karabin) = a carbine.

«Лимонка» (limonka) = a nickname for the Soviet **Ф-1** (ef-1) fragmentation antipersonnel hand grenade. Its shape resembled a lemon (in Russian – limon).

«Парабеллум» (parabellum) = the German Luger P08 Parabellum pistol.

ППД (pepede) – abbreviated **пистолет-пулемет** (pistolet-pulemiot) **Дегтярёва** = Degtiarev's 7.62mm submachine gun.

ППС (pepees) – abbreviated **пистолет-пулемет Судаева** = Sudaev's 7.62mm submachine gun.

ППШ (pepesha) – abbreviated **пистолет-пулемёт Шпагина** = Shpagin's 7.62mm submachine gun.

ПТР (peteer) – abbreviated **противотанковое ружье** (protivotankovoe ruzh'io) = an anti-tank rifle.

РГ-42 (erge-42) = the Soviet fragmentation anti-personnel hand grenade.

РПГ-43 and **РПГ-6** (erpege) = abbreviations for two main models of Soviet anti-tank grenades thrown by hand.

СВТ (esvete) – abbreviated **самозарядная винтовка** (samozariadnaia vintovka) **Токарева** = Tokarev's self-loading rifle.

СКС (eskaes) – abbreviated **самозарядный карабин** (samozariadnyi karabin) **Симонова** = Simonov's self-loading carbine.

«Суоми» (suomi) = the Finnish submachine gun "Suomi M31".

«Трёхлинейка» (triokhlineika) and **«Мосинка»** (mosinka) = two nicknames for the Russian/Soviet 7.62mm Mosin-Nagant rifle M91/30 created by S. I. Mosin in 1891; the standard rifle for the Red Army.

ТТ (tete) = an abbreviated name for Tokarev's **«Тульский»** (tul'skii) pistol.

Фауст-патрон (faust-patron) = (in German – *Panzerfaust* or "armored fist") – a handheld disposable German anti-tank weapon.

Финка (finka) = a colloquial Russian name for a dagger. Generally, the Russian word **финка** is a widespread nickname for a Finnish knife.

«Шмайссер» (shmaisser) = a widespread nickname for the German MP40 submachine gun (nicknamed by American soldiers as *the burp gun*).

Штык (shtyk) = a bayonet.

Other Weapons

Авианосец (avianosets) = an aircraft carrier.

Аэростат воздушного заграждения (aerostat vozdushnogo zagrazhdeniia) = a barrage balloon.

Броневик (bronevik) = a light armored car, equipped with a turret-mounted machine gun, and used for reconnaissance, combat support, and security.

Бронепоезд (bronepoezd) = an armored train. Usually its armored railcars were armed with guns and machine guns or housed anti-aircraft gun turrets. Germany also had fully-armored locomotives which were used on such trains.

«Ванюша» (vaniusha) = an affectionate name for Ivan; **«Иван Грозный»** (Ivan Groznyi) – Ivan the Terrible; **«скрипун»** (skripun) – a male creature who creaks; **«скрипуха»** (skripukha) – a female creature who creaks; **«ишак»** (ishak) – a donkey = nicknames for the German mobile six barrel rocket launcher *Nebelwerfer* 41. Allied soldiers nicknamed that rocket launcher the *Screaming Meemie*.

Вертолёт (vertoliot) = a helicopter.

«Гайка» (gaika) = a tank crew nickname for the tank T-34/76 (1943) tank because of its hexagonal turret. Literally **гайка** means *a nut*.

Гаубица (gaubitsa) = a howitzer.

«Дегтярёв» (degtiariov) = a nickname for two light machine guns – the original model **ДП** (dep**e**) and the modernized model **ДПМ** (dep**ee**m), both invented and modernized by V. A. Degtiarev.

«Дивизионка» (divizi**o**nka) = a nickname for the Soviet 76mm divisional gun **ЗИС-3** (zis-3); also the nickname given to the divisional weekly small newspapers that circulated at the front.

ДШК (deshek**a**) = an abbreviation for **крупнокалиберный пулемёт Дегтярёва-Шпагина** (krupnokali**b**er**h**yi pulem**io**t degtiari**o**va-shp**a**gina) which means the Degtiarev-Shpagin's large-caliber machine gun. It was often used as a light anti-aircraft machine gun.

«Зенитка» (zen**i**tka) = a nickname for any antiaircraft gun or machine gun.

«Ишак» (ishak) and **ишачок** (ishach**o**k) = nicknames for the Red Army's fighter aircraft, the Polikarpov **И-16** (I-16). Literally **ишак** means *a donkey* and **ишачок** means *a little donkey.*

«Катюша» (kati**u**sha) = a nickname for a multi-barreled rocket launcher which equipped so-called Guards Mortar units and detachments. Literally **Катюша** is *an affectionate nickname for a woman whose name is* **Екатерина** (iekater**i**na). German soldiers called the **«Катюша»** *Stalin's organ* (a large musical wind instrument).

Корвет (korv**e**t) = a corvette.

«Кукурузник» (kuku**ru**znik) = a nickname for a light night bomber **У-2ВС** (U-2VS) created under N. N. Polikarpov's supervision. Literally **кукурузник** means *somebody/something pertaining to* **кукуру**за (kuku**ru**za), which is Russian for the corn plant. The nickname for the U-2 had been given to it for its hedge-hopping flight at the same height as that of the corn. The Germans damned the **кукурузник** and called it *Rußcarton* and *Rußfaner,* meaning *Russian cardboard* and *Russian plywood* respectively.

ЛаГГ-3 (lagg-3) = the Soviet WW II fighter. **ЛаГГ** is a Russian acronym of the designers' names Lavochkin, Gorbunov, and Gudkov. The aircraft's airframe was almost completely made of timber, with crucial parts processed with Bakelite lacquer. Because of its heavy wooden and laminate construction that reduced its maneuverability, Soviet pilots jokingly interpreted **ЛаГГ** as **лакированный гарантированный гроб** (lakir**o**vannyi garant**i**rovannyi grob) that means *a lacquered guaranteed coffin.*

«Летающий танк» (let**a**iushchii tank) = a Russian nickname for S. V. Il'iushin's heavily-armored ground attack aircraft **Ил-2** (il-dva). For its striking effectiveness German soldiers nicknamed the **Ил-2** in German *Schwarz Tod* ("Black death"). Literally **летающий танк** means *a flying tank.*

«Максим» (maksim) = a nickname for the heavy machine gun invented by Hiram Maxim.

МГ-34 (emge-34) = an abbreviation for the widespread German belt-fed machine gun.

«Мессер» (messer) = a shortened name for the German Messerschmitt Me-109 fighter.

Минный тральщик (minnyi tral'shchik) = a minesweeper.

Миномёт (minomiot) = a mortar (see also **«самовар»** below). The word-for-word translation of the Russian compound word **миномёт** is *a mine launcher*.

«Музыкант» (muzykant) = a nickname for the German dive bomber Ju 87.

This nickname was given for the Ju 87's infamous wailing siren. Another nickname **«карусель»** (karusel') was given to the Ju 87 squadron's diving maneuver that resembled a merry-go-round (a carousel). Literally **музыкант** means *a musician*.

Red Army air crews nicknamed the Ju 87 **«лапоть»** (lapot') which means *a bast shoe* (a kind of footwear). This nickname was given for the outline of the Ju 87's undercarriage fairing that resembled a bast shoe.

Орудие (orudie) and **пушка** (pushka) = a gun, a cannon.

«Пешка» (peshka) = a nickname for Petliakov's **Пе-2** (pe-dva) bomber. While diving, it performed a manevuer similar to how the Ju 87 dived. Soviet airmen nicknamed that manevuer **вертушка** (vertushka). Literally **пешка** means *a chess pawn*.

Подводная лодка (podvodnaia lodka) = a submarine.

«Полковушка» (polkovushka) = a nickname for the Soviet 76mm regimental field gun (Model 1927/39).

Постановщик морских мин (postanovshchik morskikh min) = a minelayer.

ПТО (peteo) = an abbreviation for **противотанковое орудие** (protivotankovoe orudie) which means *an anti-tank gun*.

«Рама» (rama) = a nickname for the Focke-Wulf Fw-189 German reconnaissance plane (its outline resembled a frame because of its twin booms). This plane was also nicknamed **«Фокер»** (foker). Literally **рама** means *a frame*.

«Самовар» (samovar) = a nickname for **миномёт** (see above). Literally **самовар** means *a Russian tea urn with an internal heating device and an external tin pipe* and the mortar's removable barrel resembled that tin pipe.

«Самоходка» (samokhodka) – a nickname for **самоходная артиллерийская установка** (samokhodnaia artilleriiskaia ustanovka) abbreviated as **САУ** (sau) – literally *a self-propelled artillery mount* = a self-propelled gun.

The main model of Soviet **САУ**s was the **СУ-76** (su-sem'desiat shest'), often known in the West as the SU-76. Its engine operated on aircraft fuel which made the **СУ-76** highly flammable. Therefore its crews created a bitter nickname abbreviation for their self-propelled gun, namely, **БМ-4А** (beem-chetyre a) which is a Russian acronym for *fraternal grave for four artillerymen*. Another nickname for the **СУ-76** was **«сука»** (suka) which means *a bitch*.

СБ АНТ-40 – abbreviated **Скоростной бомбардировщик АНТ-40** (skorostnoi bombardirovshchik aente 40) = Tupolev's high-speed bomber.

«Сорокапятка» (sorokapiatka) = a nickname for the Soviet 45mm anti-tank gun.

«Сотка» (sotka) = a nickname for the Soviet long-barreled 100mm tank gun D-10.

Сторожевой катер (storozhevoi kater) = a patrol boat.

«Тигр» (tigr) = the German heavy tank Pz.Kpfw. VI "Tiger I".

«Фердинанд» (ferdinand) = the Ferdinand, the German heavy assault gun/tank destoyer. (Note that Red Army soldiers often referred to any German tank destroyer or self-propelled gun as a "Ferdinand").

Флагман (flagman) = a flagship – the ship where the commander is running the operations.

ШКАС (shkas) = an abbreviation for Shpital'nyi-Komatitskii's aircraft rapid-fire machine gun.

Штурмовик (shturmovik) = a ground-attack aircraft.

«Эмка» (emka) = a nickname for the name of the first Soviet car M-1 or "Molotovets-1."

Эсминец (esminets) = a destroyer.

«Ястребок» (iastrebok) = an affectionate nickname for any Soviet fighter plane. (The word **ястребок** in Russian pronunciation is fairly consonant with the word **истребитель** [istrebitel'] which means *a fighter plane*). Literally **ястребок** is *a pet name for a small or young hawk.*

6

Ammunition

Болванка (bolvanka) = a solid anti-tank shot or shot shell.

Бомба (bomba) = a bomb.

Бронебойный снаряд (broneboinyi snariad) = an armor-piercing shell.

Бутылка с зажигательной смесью (butylka s zazhigatel'noy smes'iu) = a bottle filled with an incendiary mixture, also known nowadays as a Molotov cocktail.

«Дура» (dura) = a nickname for any extra large shell or bomb. Literally **дура** means *a silly woman*.

«Зажигалка» (zazhigalka) = a nickname for any of incendiary devices or incendiary bombs. Literally **зажигалка** means *a lighter* (a device for lighting cigarettes etc.)

Зажигательный снаряд (zazhigatel'nyi snariad) = an incendiary shell.

Картечь (kartech') = case shot.

Кумулятивный снаряд (kumuliativnyi snariad) = a hollow-charge shell.

Осколочный снаряд (oskolochnyi snariad) = a fragmentation shell.

Патрон (patron) = a cartridge.

Подводная магнитная мина (podvodnaia magnitnaia mina) = an underwater magnetic mine.

Подводная мина (podvodnaia mina) = a moored underwater mine.

Противопехотная мина (protivopekhotnaia mina) = an anti-personnel land mine, a land mine.

Противотанковая авиабомба (ПТАБ) (protivotankovaia aviabomba) = an anti-tank bomb.

Противотанковая мина (protivotankovaia mina) = an antitank land mine.

Прыгающая мина (prygaiushchaia mina) = a jumping or bounding land mine known by the American soldiers as the "Bouncing Betty". When triggered, the mine would launch into the air and then detonate above ground, scattering fragments.

Пуля (pulia) = a bullet.

Разрывная пуля (razryvnaia pulia) = an explosive bullet.

РС (eres) – an abbreviation for **реактивный снаряд** (reaktivnyi snariad) = a rocket shell.

Снаряд (snariad) = a shell.

Трассирующая пуля (trassiruiushchaia pulia) = a tracer bullet.

«Фонарь» (fonar'), **«Светильник»** (svetil'nik), **«Лампада»** (lampada) = nicknames for the German illumination flare which was provided with a small parachute to slow its rate of fall and keep the area under illumination for a longer period of time. Literally **фонарь** means *a lantern*; **светильник** means *a lamp*; **лампада** means *an icon-lamp.*

Фугасная авиабомба (ФАБ) (fugasnaia aviabomba [fab]) = a high-explosive aircraft bomb.

Шрапнель (shrapnel') = shrapnel. (**«Шрапнель»** is also a Russian nickname for a pearl barley hot cereal).

7

Uniforms

Бескозырка (beskozyrka) = a sailor's cap. Literally – a peakless cap.

Ботинки солдатские (botinki soldatskie) = combat boots.

Будённовка (budionnovka) = a soft woolen hat resembling a spiked helmet. The **будённовка** was generally used by Red Army men from 1919 to 1941.

Б/У and **б/у** (beu) – abbreviations of **бывший в употреблении** (byvshii v upotreblenii) = secondhand (particularly, soldier's uniforms and underwear during the war).

Бушлат (bushlat) = a sailor's jacket, a pea-jacket.

Валенки (valenki) = felt boots.

Ватные брюки (vatnyie briuki) = quilted trousers.

Гимнастёрка (gimnastiorka) = a military blouse.

Защитный цвет (zashchitnyi tsvet) = khaki color.

Зимняя шапка (zimniaia shapka), **ушанка** (ushanka), and **треух** (treukh) = names for a winter cap with ear-flaps and back flap.

Кальсоны (kal'sony) = drawers.

Китель (kitel') = a military jacket.

Кожаная куртка лётчика (kozhanaia kurtka liotchika) = a pilot's leather jacket.

Комбинезон (kombinezon) = overalls, a jumpsuit.

Кубанка (kubanka) = a low fur cap.

Маскхалат (maskhalat) = abbreviated **маскировочный халат** (maskirovochnyi khalat) – camouflage overalls. There were winter white overalls and summer khaki ones.

Нательная рубаха (natel'naia rubakha) = an undershirt.

Нижнее бельё (nizhneio bel'io) = underclothes.

Обмотки (obmotki) = external foot-bindings wrapped around the legs from ankle to knee, a Russian version of puttees.

Обмундирование (obmundirovanie) = uniform.

Папаха (papakha) = a tall fur cap.

Парадная форма одежды (paradnaia forma odezhdy) = full-dress or parade dress uniform.

Перчатки (perchatki) = gloves.

Пилотка (pilotka) = a field service cap, resembling a side cap. Literally **пилотка** means *a pilot's cap.*

Плащ-палатка (plashch-palatka) = a waterproof cape. Literally **плащ-палатка** means *a cape-tent.*

Повседневная форма одежды (povsednevnaia forma odezhdy) = daily duty dress.

Подворотничок (podvorotnichok) = a narrow ribbon of white cotton cloth sewn on the inside of a collar so that, after the military blouse or the jacket with a stand-up collar is put on, only a tiny strip of the white cotton cloth peeps out over the collar.

Подшлемник (podshlemnik) = a woolen lining for wearing under a helmet.

Полевая форма одежды (polevaia forma odezhdy) = field dress, combat dress.

Полушубок (polushubok) = a short fur coat.

Портянки (portianki) = footcloths (wrapped around feet and ankles before putting on boots).

Рвань (rvan'), **лохмотья**, (lokhmot'ia) and **тряпьё** (triap'io) = ragged or tattered clothing.

Роба (roba) = a coverall.

Рукавицы (rukavitsy) and **варежки** (varezhki) = mittens.

Сапоги кирзовые (sapogi kirzovye) = boots made of an artificial leather.

Сапоги хромовые (sapogi khromovye) = calfskin boots.

Сапоги яловые (sapogi ialovye) = cowskin boots.

«Сидор» (sidor) = a nickname for a rucksack. Literally **Сидор** is a Russian first name of a man.

Телогрейка (telogreika) = a quilted jacket. Literally **телогрейка** means *something that warms the body.*

Тельняшка (tel'niashka) = a sailor's striped vest.

Унты (unty) = high fur boots.

Фуражка (furazhka) = a uniform cap. Literally **фуражка** means *a peak-cap.*

Хаки (khaki) [1] = a dense brownish-green fabric, khaki.

Хаки [2] = the color of **Хаки** [1].

Х/Б and **x/б** (khabe) = abbreviated **хлопчатобумажный** (khlopchatobumazhnyi) = anything made of cotton.

Хлястик (khliastik) = the rear half-belt component of a military overcoat.

Шинель (shinel') = a military overcoat.

Ширинка (shirinka) = a fly front – a closure in the front of a pair of trousers.

Шмотки (shmotki) = a slang for garments.

8

Rank Insignia

Prior to 1943

Петлицы (petlitsy) = a pair of lengthwise tabs on the collar of the military blouse, jacket, overcoat.

Three forms of metallic insignia below were to be fastened to the tabs

Прямоугольники (priamougol'niki) = rectangles. Their colloquial name was **шпалы** (shpaly) which means *ties*. The rectangles were badges of rank for the higher and highest levels of officers: 1 tie for a captain; 2 ties for a major; 3 ties for a lieutenant colonel; 4 ties for a colonel.

Квадраты (kvadraty) = squares. Their colloquial names were **кубики** (kubiki) and **кубари** (kubari), both mean *small cubes*. The squares were badges of rank for mid-rank officers: 1 square for a junior lieutenant; 2 squares for a lieutenant; 3 squares for a senior lieutenant.

Треугольники (treugol'niki) = triangles that were badges of rank for NCOs: 1 triangle for a corporal; 2 triangles for a junior sergeant; 3 triangles for a sergeant; 4 triangles for a sergeant major. The vulgar but widespread nickname for such a triangle was **секиль** (sekil') which means *clitoris*.

After 1943

Погоны (pogony) = a pair of narrow, stiff, cloth patches worn on the shoulders by soldiers, NCOs, officers and generals.

Лычки (lychki) = the NCOs' badges of rank, cross strips on the **погоны** (above): 1 narrow strip for a corporal; 2 narrow strips for a junior sergeant; 3 narrow strips for a sergeant; 1 wide strip for a senior sergeant; 1 wide strip and 1 narrow lengthwise strip for a sergeant major.

Металлические звёздочки (metallicheskie zviozdochki) = metallic starlets that were badges of rank for mid-rank officers: 1starlet for a junior lieutenant; 2 starlets for a lieutenant; 3 starlets for a senior lieutenant; 4 starlets for a captain.

Металлические звёзды (metallicheskie zviozdy) = metallic stars that were badges of rank for the higher and highest levels of officers: 1 star for a major; 2 stars for a lieutenant colonel; 3 stars for a colonel.

Note: Insignias of rank for generals were special **погоны** (see above) and stars.

9

Decorations

Ордена (ordena) = Orders

Орден Ленина (orden lenina) = Order of Lenin. Note: Persons awarded the honorary title of **Герой Советского Союза** (geroi sovetskogo soiuza) = the Hero of the Soviet Union were simultaneously presented with the Order of Lenin and **медаль Золотая Звезда** (medal' zolotaia zvezda) – the Golden Star medal.

Орден Красного Знамени (orden krasnogo znameni) = Order of the Red Banner.

Орден Славы 1-й (2-й, 3-й) **степени** (orden slavy 1-oi [2-oi, 3-ei] stepeni) = 1st (2nd 3rd) Class Order of Glory.

Орден Суворова 1-й (2-й, 3-й) **степени** (orden Suvorova 1-oi [2-oi, 3-ei] stepeni) = 1st (2nd, 3rd) Class Order of Suvorov.

Орден Кутузова 1-й (2-й, 3-й) **степени** (orden Kutuzova 1-oi [2-oi, 3-ei] stepeni) = 1st (2nd, 3rd) Class Order of Kutuzov.

Орден Ушакова 1-й (2-й) **степени** (orden Ushakova 1-oi [2-oi] stepeni) = 1st (2nd Class Order of Ushakov.

Орден Нахимова 1-й (2-й) **степени** (orden Nakhimova 1-oi [2-oi] stepeni) = 1st (2nd) Class Order of Nakhimov.

Орден Богдана Хмельницкого 1-й (2-й, 3-й) **степени** (orden Bogdana Khmel'nitskogo 1-oi [2oi, 3-ei stepeni) = 1st (2nd, 3rd) Class Order of Bogdan Khmel'nitskii.

Орден Александра Невского (orden aleksandra nevskogo) = Order of Alexander Nevskii.

Орден Отечественной войны 1-й (2-й) **степени** (orden otechestvennoi voiny 1-oi [2-oi] stepeni) = 1st (2nd) Class Order of the Patriotic War.

Орден Красной Звезды (orden krasnoi zvezdy) = Order of the Red Star.

Медали (medali) = Medals

За отвагу (za otvagu) = For Bravery.

За боевые заслуги (za boevye zaslugi) = For Combat Merits. Note: Besides common frontline soldiers, many other categories of servicemen could be awarded with this medal: wagon drivers, stockmen, cooks, clerks etc. as well as members of medical detachments which consisted mostly of women (some of whom were at the same time some an officer's "campaign wife"). This latter circumstance served as the basis for a sarcastic nickname for this medal – **«За половые услуги»** (za polovye uslugi), which means *"For sexual services."*

Медаль Ушакова (medal' Ushakova) = Medal of Ushakov.

Медаль Нахимова (medal' Nakhimova) = Medal of Nakhimov.

Партизану Великой Отечественной войны 1-й (2-й) степени (partizanu velikoi otechestvennoi voiny 1-oi [2-oi] stepeni) = 1st (2nd) Class To a Partisan of the Great Patriotic War.

За победу над Германией в Великой Отечественной войне 1941-1945 гг. (za pobedu nad Germaniei v velikoi otechestvennoi voine 1941-1945 gg.) = For Victory over Germany in the Great Patriotic War 1941 – 1945.

За победу над Японией (za pobedu nad Iaponiei) = For Victory over Japan.

За оборону Сталинграда (za oboronu Stalingrada) = For Defense of Stalingrad.

За оборону Москвы (za oboronu Moskvy) = For Defense of Moscow.

За оборону Ленинграда (za oboronu Leningrada) = For Defense of Leningrad.

За оборону Севастополя (za oboronu Sevastopolia) = For Defense of Sevastopol'.

За оборону Одессы (za oboronu Odessy) = For Defense of Odessa.

За оборону Кавказа (za oboronu Kavkaza) = For Defense of the Caucasus.

За оборону Киева (za oboronu Kieva) = For Defense of Kiev.

За оборону Советской Арктики (za oboronu Sovetskoi Arktiki) = For Defense of the Soviet Arctic.

За взятие Кенигсберга (za vziatie Kenigsberga) = For the Capture of Königsberg.

За взятие Будапешта (za vziatie Budapeshta) = For the Capture of Budapest.

За взятие Вены (za vziatie Veny) = For the Capture of Vienna.

За взятие Берлина (za vziatie Berlina) = For the Capture of Berlin.

За освобождение Белграда (za osvobozhdenie Belgrada) = For the Liberation of Belgrade.

За освобождение Варшавы (za osvobozhdenie Varshavy) = For the Liberation of Warsaw.

За освобождение Праги (za osvobozhdenie Pragi) = For the Liberation of Prague.

A special note It is well known, that many high-ranking Red Army commanders, such as division commanders, corps commanders and higher, abused their power when it was a question of decorations. As a result, their full-dress jackets were well-covered with orders and medals. However, Leonid Brezhnev, the former leader of the USSR, had a special soft spot in his heart for decorations and his postwar collection of awards including many foreign orders and medals was absolutely enormous. People laughed at him and ironically named his collection of awards "iconostas". Literally **иконостас** (ikonostas) is *a wall in an orthodox church on which icons are placed, separating the sanctuary from the main part of the church.*

Юбилейные медали (iubileinye medali) = Anniversary medals

XX лет РККА (dvadtsat' let erkaka) = XX Anniversary of the RKKA (Workers' and Peasans' Red Army).

30 лет Советской Армии и Флота (tridtsat' let sovetskoi Armii i Flota) = 30th Anniversary of the Soviet Army and Navy.

40 лет Вооружённых Сил СССР (sorok let vooruzhionnykh sil eseseser) = 40th Anniversary of the Armed Forces of the USSR.

50 лет Вооружённых Сил СССР (piat'desiat let vooruzhionnykh sil eseseser) = 50th Anniversary of the Armed Forces of the USSR.

60 лет Вооружённых Сил СССР (shest'desiat let vooruzhionnykh sil eseseser) = 60th Anniversary of the Armed Forces of the USSR.

70 лет Вооружённых Сил СССР (sem'desiat let vooruzhionnykh sil eseseser) = 70th Anniversary of the Armed Forces of the USSR.

Довоенные оборонные значки (dovoennye oboronnye znachki) = Pre-war civil defense badges

Ворошиловский стрелок (voroshilovskii strelok) = Voroshilov's Markman.

Готов к труду и обороне (gotov k trudu i oborone) = Ready for Labor and Defense.

Готов к санитарной обороне (gotov k sanitarnoi oborone) = Ready for Medical Defense.

Готов к противовоздушной и противохимической обороне (gotov k protivovozdushnoi i protivokhimicheskoi oborone) = Ready for Anti-aircraft and Anti-chemical Defense.

10

Food, Drinks, Tobacco, etc.

Food

Баланда (balanda) = a scanty wishy-washy soup.

Жратва (zhratva) and **варево** (varevo) = demotic words for food; grub or swill.

Затеруха (zaterukha), also **затируха** (zatirukha) = in years of starvation (as during the war) – a poor soup of several small pieces of dough boiled in just water – a kind of **баланда** (see above). In general, **затеруха** is a quite palatable soup.

«Зачерпни для меня со дна пожиже» (zacherpni dlia menia so dna pozhizhe) = "Ladle for me the wateriest from the bottom." (A funny request while a soldier is handing his mess-kit to the cook).

«Кашевар» (kashevar) = a nickname for a cook. Literally **кашевар** means *a person, who cooks kasha.*

«Кому-кому» или как на передовой обычно делили буханку хлеба на четверых = "Komu-komu" or how in the frontline a round loaf was usually distributed for a group of four. After receiving the loaf, the group would place it on a towel or on a newspaper and elect one of them to be the cutter and another one to be the guesser. The first-elect quartered the loaf with a knife as precisely as possible. The three onlookers either approved the result or asked the cutter to adjust the division. Then the guesser faced away from the bread, and one of the three remaining soldiers in the group would point his finger at the pieces of bread, one at a time. Each time, while pointing at a piece, he the same question to the guesser loudly: "To whom?" (in Russian, "Kom**u**?"); in response, the guesser called out the name of a soldier, who then received this piece of bread.

Кормилец (kormilets) [1] = an affectionate name for a person (like a detachment's sergeant major or a detachment's cook), who provides soldiers with food.

Кормилец [2] = a bread-winner.

Наедаться «от пуза» (naedat'sia ot puza) and **объедаться** (obyedat'sia) = to cram oneself with food. Literally **пузо** means *a belly.*

«Сыт, пьян, и нос в табаке» (syt, p'ian, i nos v tabake) = a colloquial expression that describes a state of complete satisfaction. Literally **«Сыт, пьян, и нос в табаке»** means "[I'm] *full, drunk and with* [my] *nose into tobacco*".

Умять (umiat') = to eat up or to stuff down any food.

Alcohol

Быть «под мухой» (byt' pod mukhoi) = to be a little tipsy. Literally **быть «под мухой»** means *to be "under a fly."*

Выпивать (vypivat') = to drink (alcohol), to hit the bottle regularly.

Выпить (vypit') = to drink (alcohol) one time.

«Заложить за воротник» (zalozhit' za vorotnik) = to hit the bottle. Literally **заложить за воротник** means *to put* [something] *behind a collar.*

«Набраться» (nabrat'sia) = to get drunk completely. Literally **набраться** means *to pick up* [something] *in full measure.*

«Наркомовские сто грамм» (narkomovskie sto gramm) = a front-line nickname for the daily ration of 0.1 liter of vodka for Red Army soldiers while at the front line.

Ни в одном глазу (ni v odnom glazu) = a Russian figurative phrase that expresses a state of complete soberness. Literally **ни в одном глазу** means *in no one eye.*

«Обмывать» (obmyvat') = to celebrate (as a new acquisition, a promotion, an award etc.) with drinks. Literally **обмывать** means *to bathe* [someone/something].

Окосеть (okoset') = to get drunk. Literally **окосеть** means *to get cross-eyed.*

Похмелье (pokhmel'e) = a hangover.

Самогон (samogon) = moonshine.

Спирт (spirt) = spirits or strong liquor.

Чекушка (chekushka) = a nickname for a quarter-liter bottle of alcohol.

Чиста, как слеза Божья! (chista kak sleza bozh'ia) = As pure as God's tear! (The exclamation pertained to any colorless alcohol liquid).

A popular universal (unaddressed) toast in Ukrainian: **Будьмо!** (bud'mo), which means *"Let's be!"*

Tobacco etc.

Бычок (bychok) and **чинарик** (chinarik) = a cigarette-butt.

Дай закурить (dai zakurit') = Give me something to smoke.

Дай потянуть (day potianut') = Give me a drag off of the cigarette that you are smoking.

Дай докурить (dai dokurit') or **дай 40** (dai sorok) = Let me finish the cigarette that you are smoking.

Дай прикурить (dat' prikurit') = Give me a light from your cigarette.

Кресало (kresalo) = a device for making a fire with two pieces of flint and a thick wick.

Курево (kurevo) = something to smoke.

Махорка (makhorka) = a crude kind of Russian strong tobacco that was a part of the daily ration for soldiers assigned to the Operating Army during the war.

Папиросы (papirosy) = special Russian cigarettes with a conjunctive tubular cigarette holder made of thick paper.

Самокрутка (samokrutka) = a hand-rolled cigarette made of a piece of newsprint and any sort of tobacco including the makhorka (see above). There was also a modified version of samokrutka for makhorka, so-called **козья ножка** (koz'ia nozhka). Literally **козья ножка** means *a goat's leg*.

Самосад (samosad) = homegrown tobacco.

«Стрелять» (streliat') = to cadge a cigarette or a **самокрутка** (see above). Literally **стрелять** means *to shoot, to fire* etc.

Уши опухли (ushi opukhli) = a figurative expression that describes how an inveterate smoker suffers after not smoking for a long time. Literally **уши опухли** means [my] *ears got swollen*.

A humorous example of cadging:
Не найдётся ли у вас бумажки цигарку скрутить – я табачок и спички дома забыл? (ne naidiotsia li u vas bumazhki tsigarku skrutit' ia tabachok i spichki doma zabyl?) = Could you find a piece of newsprint for rolling a cigarette? I left my tobacco and matches at home.

11

Abbreviations

АРГК – abbreviated **Артиллерия Резерва Главного Командования** (artilleriia rezerva glavnogo komandovaniia) = Artillery of the Supreme Command Reserve.

Артмастер (artmaster) – abbreviated **артиллерийский мастер** (artilleriiskii master) = an armorer.

БАО (bao) – abbreviated **батальон аэродромного обслуживания** (batal'on aerodromnogo obsluzhivaniia) = an airfield maintenance battalion.

БАП (bap) [**БАД** (bad), **БАК** (bak)] – abbreviated **бомбардировочный авиаполк** [**бомбардировочная авиадивизия, бомбардировочный авиакорпус**] = a bomber aviation regiment [division, corps].

Боепитание (boiepitanie) – abbreviated **боевое питание** (boevoe pitanie) = Armament and Ammunition Supply Service.

ВВС (vevees) – abbreviated **Военно-воздушные силы** (voenno-vozdushnye sily) = Air Forces.

ВКП[б] (vekapebe) – abbreviated **Всесоюзная Коммунистическая Партия** [**большевиков**] (vsesoiuznaia kommunisticheskaia partiia [bol'shevikov]) = the All-Union Communist Party [bol'shevik] – the official name of the Soviet Communist Party 1925–1952.

ВЛКСМ (veelkaesem) – abbreviated official name of the **Всесоюзный Ленинский Коммунистический Союз Молодёжи** (vsesoiuznyi leninskii kommunisticheskii soiuz molodiozhi) = All-Union Leninist Young Communist League.

ВМФ (veemef) – abbreviated **Военно-морской флот** (voenno-morskoi flot) = Navy.

Военкомат (voienkomat) – abbreviated **военный комиссариат** (voiennyi kommissariat) = a military commissariat, a military registration and enlistment office.

ГлавПУР (glavpur) and **ГлавПУРККА** (glavpurkaka) – both abbreviated **Главное Политическое Управление РККА** = versions for the Main Political Directorate of the **РККА** (see below).

ДОП (dop) – abbreviated **дивизионный обменный пункт** (divizionnyi obmennyi punkt) = a division's rear ammunition depot.

Замкомбат (zamkombat) [1] = abbreviated deputy battalion commander.

Замкомбат [2] = abbreviated deputy battery commander.

Замполит (zampolit) = abbreviated deputy for political affairs.

ИАП (iap) [**ИАД** (iad), **ИАК** (iak)] – abbreviated **истребительный авиаполк** [**истребительная авиадивизия, истребительный авиакорпус**] = a fighter aviation regiment [division, corps].

Кавторанг (kavtorang) = *(WW I)* abbreviated 2nd class captain (see Chapter 2).

Каперанг (kaperang) = *(WW I)* abbreviated 1st class captain (see Chapter 2).

КГБ (kagebe) – abbreviated **Комитет Государственной Безопасности** (komitet gosudarstvennoi bezopasnosti) = the National Security Committee.

Командарм (komandarm) – abbreviated **командующий армией** (komanduiushchii armiei) = army commander.

Комбат (kombat) [1] – abbreviated **командир батальона** (komandir batal'ona) = battalion commander.

Комбат [2] – abbreviated **командир батареи** (komandir batarei) = battery commander.

Комбриг (kombrig) – abbreviated **командир бригады** (komandir brigady) = brigade commander.

Комдив (komdiv) – abbreviated **командир дивизии** (komandir divizii) = division commander.

Комкор (komkor) – abbreviated **командир корпуса** (komandir korpusa) = corps commander.

Комсомол (komsomol) – abbreviated **Коммунистический союз молодёжи** (kommunisticheskii soiuz molodiozhi) = the everyday name of the **ВЛКСМ** (see above).

Комсомолец (komsomolets) = a **комсомол** (see above) member.

Комсорг (komsorg) – abbreviated **комсомольский организатор** (komsomol'skii organizator) = an elected or appointed leader, organizer of a group of several **комсомол** (see above) members.

Комсостав (komsostav) – abbreviated **командирский состав** (komandirskii sostav) = the military command staff.

Комэск (komesk) [1] – abbreviated **командир эскадрильи** (komandir eskadril'i) = commander of an air squadron.

Комэск [2] – abbreviated **командир эскадрона** (komandir eskadrona) = commander of a cavalry squadron.

Матчасть – abbreviated **материальная часть** (material'naia chast') = equipment.

Медсанбат (medsanbat) – abbreviated **медико-санитарный батальон** (mediko-sanitarnyi batal'on) = a medical-sanitary battalion.

Нарком (narkom) – abbreviated **Народный Комиссар** (narodnyi komissar) = the People's Commissar (a Minister).

Наркомат (narkomat) – abbreviated **Народный Комиссариат** (narodnyi komissariat) = the People's Commissariat (a Ministry).

Начарт (nachart) – abbreviated **начальник артиллерии** (nachal'nik artillerii) = chief of artillery.

Начсвязи (nachsviazi) – abbreviated **начальник связи** (nachal'nik sviazi) = chief signal officer.

Начхим (nachkhim) – abbreviated **начальник химической службы** (nachal'nik khimicheskoi sluzhby) = chief of the chemical service.

Начфин (nachfin) – abbreviated **начальник финансовой службы** (nachal'nik finansovoi sluzhby) = chief of the finance service.

Начштаба (nachshtaba) – abbreviated **начальник штаба** (nachal'nik shtaba) = chief of staff (HQ).

НКВД (enkavede) – abbreviated **Народный Комиссариат Внутренних Дел** (narodnyi komissariat vnutrennikh del) = the Ministry of Internal Affairs.

НКО (enkao) – abbreviated **Народный Комиссариат Обороны** (narodnyi komissariat oborony) = the Ministry of Defense.

ОВС (ovees) – abbreviated **обозно-вещевое снабжение** (obozno-veshchevoe snabzhenie) = the Wagon Train and Clothing Supply Service.

Осоавиахим (osoaviakhim) – abbreviated **Общество содействия обороне, авиационному и химическому строительству** (obshchestvo sodeistviia oborone aviatsionnomu i khimicheskomu stroitel'stvu) = the Society of Assistance to the Defense, Aircraft and Chemical Industry Development.

Партком (partkom) – abbreviated **партийный комитет** (partiinyi komitet) = a Communist Party Committee.

Парткомиссия (partkomissiia) – abbreviated **партийная комиссия** (partiinaia komissiia) = a Communist Party commission.

Парторг (partorg) – abbreviated **партийный организатор** (partiinyi organizator) = an elected or appointed leader, organizer of a group of several Communist Party members.

ПВО (peveo) – abbreviated **противовоздушная оборона** (protivovozdushnaia oborona) = anti-aircraft defense. There were both **ПВО** anti-aircraft artillery units and **ПВО** aviation units (the latter operated alongside the **ВВС** units [see above]).

ПНШ (peensha) – abbreviated **помощник начальника штаба** (pomoshchnik nachal'nika shtaba) = assistant chief of staff (HQ).

Политбюро (politbiuro) – abbreviated **политическое бюро** (politicheskoe biuro) = the Political Bureau – the highest governing body of the Soviet Communist Party.

Политработник (politrabotnik) – abbreviated **политический работник** (politicheskii rabotnik) = a political worker.

Политрук (politruk) – abbreviated **политический руководитель** (politicheskii rukovoditel') = a deputy commander for political affairs; a political instructor.

ППГ (pepege) – abbreviated **полевой передвижной госпиталь** (polevoi peredvizhnoi gospital') = a mobile field hospital.

Помкомвзвода (pomkomvzvoda) – abbreviated **помощник командира взвода** (pomoshchnik komandira vzvoda) = assistant platoon commander.

ПТАД (ptad) – abbreviated **противотанковый артиллерийский дивизион** (protivotankovyi artilleriiskii division) = an antitank artillery battalion.

ПТО (peteo) – abbreviated **противотанковая оборона** (protivotankovaia oborona) = antitank defense.

ПУАЗО (puazo) – abbreviated **прибор управления артиллерийским зенитным огнём** (pribor upravleniia artilleriiskim zenitnym ogniom) = a device for controlling an anti-aircraft gun.

ПФС (pefees) = abbreviation for the Food and Forage Supply Service.

РККА (erkaka) – abbreviated **Рабоче-Крестьянская Красная Армия** (raboche-krest'ianskaia krasnaia armiia) = the Worker's and Peasant's Red Army.

СМЕРШ (smersh) = an abbreviation for the Russian phrase «**Смерть шпионам!**» (smert' shpionam), which means *"Death to spies!"* The **СМЕРШ** administration, departments, detachments, and groups were established in April 1943 as a Red Army counterespionage institution. Its predecessors were the «**Особые отделы**» (osobye otdely) = Special Departments that were under the Ministry of Internal Affairs.

There were in the **СМЕРШ** structure small detachments (usually squads), which executed the capital punishments. Members of these detachments were called «**расстрельщики**» (rasstrel'shchiki) – those who execute by shooting. More often soldiers of the unit's commandant's platoon performed the execution.

Совинформбюро (sovinformbiuro) – abbreviated **Советское информационное бюро** (sovetskoie informatsionnoie biuro) = the leading Soviet news agency during the war. It was established by a directive of the **Совнарком** (see below) and the Central Committee of the **ВКП[б]** (see above) "to bring into the limelight international events, military developments, and day-to-day life through printed and broadcast media."

Совнарком (sovnarkom) – abbreviated **Совет народных комиссаров** (sovet narodnykh komissarov) = the Council of People's Commissars, i. e. the USSR government.

ЦИК (tsik) – abbreviated **Центральный Исполнительный Комитет** (tsentral'nyi ispolnitel'nyi komitet) = the Central Executive Committee, a likeness of a legislative body in the prewar USSR.

ЦК (tseka) – abbreviated **центральный комитет** (tsentral'nyi komitet) = a central committee of an official institution or organization. In the USSR, the term **ЦК** without its specification usually stood for the Central Committee of the **ВКП(б)** (see above).

ШАП (shap) [**ШАД** (shad), **ШАК** (shak)] – abbreviated **штурмовой авиаполк [авиадивизия, авиакорпус]** = an assault or ground attack aviation regiment [division, corps].

12

Wartime Terms, Sayings and Colloquial Expressions

Автоматчик (avtomatchik) = a submachine gunner.

Адъютант (adiutant) = a staff officer attached to a superior commander as a principal aide. (See also **порученец** below).

Аттестат (attestat) – a colloquial form of **денежный аттестат** (denezhnyi attestat) = a part of an officer's money allowance that he/she addressed to his/her family through the local military registration and enlistment office.

Аттестат на продовольствие (attestat na prodovol'stvie) = a food certificate for a serviceman/servicewoman, who had an authorized leave of absence or was being transferred to a different unit/garrison. The certificate's holder had the opportunity to be served free of charge at any military canteen or at any grocery store subordinated to the Ministry of Defense.

«Белобилетник» (belobiletnik) = a "white card" holder (a person exempted from military service).

Боец (boets) [1] = an informal name for a private, a soldier.

Боец [2] = a combatant, a fighter, a warrior.

Броня (bronia) = colloquial name for the status of being exempted from military service without regard for age or medical history. Literally **броня** (bronia) means *armor*

«Буржуйка» (burzhuika) = a small cylindrical metal oven (often homemade).

Вахта (vakhta) = a watch, as in a sailors' or Marines' period of duty.

Вахтенный (vakhtennyi) = a sailor or a Marine on duty.

Верховой (verkhovoi) and **всадник** (vsadnik) = a rider, a horseman.

Взводный (vzvodnyi) = (*WW I*) a colloquial name for a platoon commander.

Виллис (villis) = Willys – an American jeep. Numerous jeeps were delivered from the USA to the USSR as a part of the American lend-lease program of assistance to the USSR.

Военное лихолетье (voennoe likholet'e) = times of war-related disasters.

«Война всё спишет» (voina vsio spishet) = the war would write off (concede, excuse) anything (including any inhuman, illegal and unjust actions). Being guided by such an all-permissive promise, many people, especially authorities and commanders, did whatever they wanted to do without regard for legality or scruples.

Вошебойка (vosheboika) = a self-made arrangement for killing lice by heat-treating. (See also **санпропускник** below).

«Выковыренный» (vykovyrennyi) = a scornful nickname for **эвакуированный** (see below). Literally **выковыренный** means *something picked out from within a dense medium.*

Гвардеец (gvardeets) = a member of any Soviet Guards military unit (the honorific Guards title usually was given to a unit for a series of successful battles).

«Гражданка» (grazhdanka) = civilian life or "Civvy Street." Literally **гражданка** means *a female citizen.*

«Губа» (guba) = a nickname for **гауптвахта** (gauptvakhta) that means a guardroom. Literally **губа** means *a lip.*

Дневальный (dneval'nyi) = a soldier on duty in a barrack.

Ездовой (ezdovoi) = a driver of a horse-drawn carriage or horse-drawn limber.

Заряжающий (zariazhaiushchii) = a loader.

Кавалерист (kavalerist) = a cavalryman.

Камбуз (kambuz) = a ship's galley.

Карательные отряды (karate'nye otriady) = German special military police commands in the occupied territory of the USSR. They searched for Soviet partisan and underground groups, as well as for communists and Jews. Their goal was to annihilate or at least to arrest all of their enemies. Literally **карательные отряды** means *punitive commands* or *punitive detachments.*

Караульный (karaul'nyi) and **часовой** (chasovoi) = a sentry.

Карточки (kartochki) = a colloquial name for the food ration cards that all Soviet urban citizen carried during the war. The food quotas, especially for bread, fat, meat, and sugar, were extremely small.

Комиссовать (komissovat') = an informal word that means to determine the person's reason to avoid military service and, if needed, to resolve the category of his/her disability.

«Кому война, а кому – мать родна» (komu voina a komu mat' rodna) = "To some it is war, while for others it is like their own mother." This folk wisdom was aimed at those who profited from the wartime conditions. It was very popular during the war not only in the rear but also at the front.

«Кому война – верёвка, а кому – дойная коровка» (komu voina veriovka a komu doinaia korovka) = "To some the war is like a noose [around their necks], while for others it is like a dairy cow." (In Russian pronunciation the phrase is rhymed). This is another folk reference to war-time profiteers.

Коптилка (koptilka) and **плошка** (ploshka) = a primitive hand-crafted wick lamp.

Лазарет (lazaret) = (*WW I*) a colloquial name for a small field hospital or medical detachment.

«ЛИКБЕЗ» (likbez) – an abbreviation for **ликвидация безграмотности** (likvidatsiia bezgramotnosti), the name of the Soviet nation-wide program for reducing illiteracy among the Soviet people inherited from the Russian empire = a colloquial figurative (sometimes with a shade of irony) term which means teaching someone who is untrained or at least insufficiently trained. For example, a company commander instructs his subordinate platoon commander: *"You should organize a good «ЛИКБЕЗ» for these three clumsy soldiers who just joined your platoon – they are absolutely unready for action!"*

Наводчик (navodchik) = a gunlayer, the member of a gun crew who aims the gun at a target.

Наряд (nariad) [1] = a commission (not a combat one) to be executed according to a roster or a particular temporary duty given to servicemen by commanders. **Наряд вне очереди** (nariad vne ocheredi) means an additional duty given as a punishment for some violation.

Наряд [2] = fine clothes.

На фронт не набивайся, от фронта не отбивайся (na front ne nabivaisia, ot fronta ne otbivaisia) = a rhymed wise saying which could be interpreted in two following ways:

[1] *Don't struggle to get to the front* [but at the same time] *don't struggle to avoid it.*
[2] *Don't volunteer, but also don't shirk if you are called.*

Нацмен (natsmen) = a colloquial term for a person belonging to one of many ethnic minorities of the USSR.

«Огневик» (ognevik) = a member of a cannon platoon.

Оправиться! [1] (opravit'sia) = a command given to the members of a unit's/detachment's formation for putting their individual weapon and uniform in a proper order.

Оправиться [2] = a part of a colloquial command given to a marching column when it should be stopped for a short halt. The full command could sound: **«КОЛОННА, короткий привал! Оправиться и покурить!»** (kolonna korotkii prival opravit'sia i pokurit') that could be translated as *"COLUMN! Short halt! Relieve yourselves and have a smoke!"*

Ординарец (ordinarets), **вестовой** (vestovoi) [*WW I*], **денщик** (denshchik) [*WW I*] and **посыльный** (posyl'nyi) = an orderly.

«Особист» (osobist), **«особняк»** (osobniak) and **«смершевец»** = nicknames for the officers and other servicemen/servicewomen of the **«Особые отделы»** and for the **СМЕРШ** groups (see the **СМЕРШ** definition in Chapter 11). Literally **особняк** means *a mansion*.

Отделённый (otdelionnyi) = (*WW I*) a colloquial name for a squad commander.

Пехотинец (pekhotinets) = an infantryman, a rifleman.

Платформа (platforma) = an open flatcar (there are more meanings of this noun).

Повозочный (povozochnyi) = a wagoner, a wagon driver.

«Полевая почта 19637- Л» (polevaia pochta 19637- el) = an example of how mail was addressed to a frontline soldier during the war. The five-digit number represented the coded number of a certain unit, and the Russian letter at the end of the address represented a particular detachment of that unit. (Specifically 19637 represented the 261st Guards Rifle Regiment, and the **Л** letter stood for the commandant's platoon of that regiment). Literally **полевая почта** means *field postal service*.

Подносчик снарядов (podnoschik snariadov) = a shell carrier, the member of a gun crew who carries shells to the gun emplacement.

Подписка на заём (podpiska na zaiom) = a subscription to a yearly Soviet government loan. During the war all the Red Army officers signed up for a sum no less than their monthly allowance.

Полицай (politsai) = a policeman – a member of a local police group in Soviet villages and towns under occupation by German troops. Usually the German commandant appointed local young men to be policemen. Most of them were loyal to Germans and cruel to local residents. Often these policemen participated in the punitive detachments (see **Карательные отряды** above).

Note: The name of the Soviet (now Russian) police is **милиция** (militsia). It is a State institution.

Порученец (poruchenets) = a special messenger, an officer subordinated to a high ranked officer.

«Посиделки» (posidelki) = a typical occasion for leisurely sharing a good dose of alcohol by a small group of front-line officers in a non-combat situation. These **«посиделки»** were an approved way to dispel homesickness and the tension of combat. Usually lively conversations and folk songs accompanied these meetings. Literally **«посиделки»** can be interpreted as *a "sit-together time."*

Посудина (posudina) = a figurative word for a ship, a boat etc. Literally **посудина** means *a large dish or a saucepan.*

Похоронка (pokhoronka) = a colloquial name for the official notice about a soldier's or officer's death.

Разбить наголову (razbit' nagolovu) and **разгромить** (razgromit') = to defeat (enemy troops) totally; to smash, batter or inflict a drubbing.

Разведчик (razvedchik) [1] = a scout, a recon.

Разведчик [2] = an intelligence officer.

Ротный (rotnyi) = (*WW I*) a colloquial name for a company commander.

Самоволка (samovolka) = a colloquial term for an unauthorized absence (known in the USA as AWOL).

Самострел (samostrel) = a man, who deliberately inflicted a wound to himself in order to leave the front line. Any uncovered **самострел** was sent before a military tribunal trial. As a rule, he was shot in front of the unit's formation or escorted to the penal detachment (see **штрафная рота** and **штрафной батальон** below).

Санитар/санитарка (sanitar/sanitarka) = a male/female medical orderly.

Санпропускник (sanpropusknik) – abbreviated **санитарный пропускник** (sanitarnyi propusknik) = a sanitary-disinfection complex that consisted of a heat-treating disinfection section for the outer clothing, uniform and underwear and a bath section for the visitors. During the war such complexes were arranged at any sizable railroad station and port. All arrivals, both individuals and groups, were to undergo the full sanitary process there. A special certificate given by the complex after a person or group had been processed was a compulsory document to stay in a city or settlement. The nationwide system of these complexes averted a typhus epidemic in the USSR during the war.

Сельский староста (sel'skii starosta) = a village headman. The German occupiers appointed a village headman in each village of the occupied zone of the USSR (instead of a former head of the Village Soviet). Some of these appointees were loyal to the German rule with all their hearts, others just pretended to be loyal.

Сестра (sestra) = a colloquial term for **медицинская сестра** (meditsinskaia sestra) = a female nurse. Literally **сестра** means a sister. Injured soldiers, while being treated in hospitals, used affectionate versions of **сестра** – **сестричка** (sestrichka) and **сестрёнка** (sestrionka) – when they requested a female nurse/medical orderly.

Солдафон (soldafon) = a scornful name for a long-time NCO/officer who is lacking in culture and is a narrow-minded person.

Склянка (sklianka) = a bell – any of the half-hour units of nautical time rung on the bell of a ship.

«Студер» (studer) and **«Парень с ветерком»** (paren' s veterkom) = two nicknames for a Studebaker truck. Literally **парень с ветерком** means *a guy with the wind* (because of its high speed movement).

«Стукач» (stukach) = a nickname for a covert informant. Literally **стукач** means *a person who knocks on a door.*

Тыловик (tylovik) = a person who serves in any detachment of the rear services.

Факельщик (fakelshchik) = a colloquial name for a member of a German incendiary command which set houses on fire before the occupiers' retreating from a settlement. Literally **факельщик** means *a torch-bearer.*

Фонд обороны (fond oborony) = the Defense Fund in the USSR that arose in December 1942 through the mass voluntary donations made by Soviet people. Among different forms of donations there were both individual and collective forms, such as individual monthly one-day-salary-deductions and a collective unpaid work on Sundays etc. The means collected by the Defense Fund were spent to construct over 2,500 aircraft for the Soviet Air Forces, eight submarines etc.

«Штамповка» (shtampovka) = a Russian nickname for the cheapest German die-cast watches. (It was a custom among Soviet troops to remove any watch, most of which proved to be die-cast ones, from any German, when the front line reached Germany).

Штрафная рота (shtrafnaia rota) and **штрафной батальон** (shtrafnoi batal'on) or shortened **штрафбат** (shtrafbat) = the Red Army penal detachments consisting of servicemen guilty of some heinous crime or misdeed (such as a refusal or non-fulfillment of a combat order; desertion, cowardice in fighting etc.) These detachments were sent to fight on the most dangerous sectors of the front and given the most dangerous assignments such as spearheading attacks. Their soldiers were eligible for commutation of the sentence (early release) and re-assignment to a Red Army line units if they either suffered a combat injury (the crime was considered to be "redeemed with blood") or performed extremely heroic deeds in combat.

«Штрафник» (shtrafnik) = a colloquial name for a member of a penal detachment. Literally **штрафник** is a colloquial name for a person who has been fined.

Эвакуированный (evakuirovannyi) = an evacuee.

Some Soviet Political Propaganda Wartime Slogans & Clichés

Артиллерия – бог войны (artilleriia – bog voiny) = Artillery is the God of war.

Всё для фронта, всё для победы над врагом! (vsio dlia fronta vsio dlia pobedy nad vragom) = Everything – for the front, everything – for victory over the enemy (Thousands of such posters were exhibited in every collective farm, plant or factory in the Soviet far rear).

Гвардия не отступает и не сдаётся (gvardiia ne otstupaed i ne sdaiotsia) = The Guards don't retreat and don't surrender.

Где гвардия наступает – враг не устоит (gde gvardiia nastupaet – vrag ne ustoit) = Where the Guards are attacking – the enemy can't stand fast.

Единственная привилегия члена партии – быть впереди в боях за Родину = The only [Communist] Party member's privilege – is to be in front while fighting for the Motherland.

За нашу Советскую Родину! (za nashu sovetskuiu rodinu) = For our Soviet Motherland!

За Родину, за Сталина! (za rodinu, za Stalina) = For the Motherland, for Stalin!

Защитники Родины (zashchitniki rodiny) = The Motherland's defenders. This term related to all the soldiers and officers who fought at the front.

Отступать некуда – за нами Москва! (otstupat' nekuda – za nami Moskva) = There is nowhere to retreat – Moscow is behind us!

Родина-мать зовёт! (rodina-mat' zoviot) = The Motherland calls! (This was a color poster where the text was placed above a picture of a middle-aged woman clothed in red who is making an appeal to the viewers. Millions of such posters were exhibited in all settlements of the Soviet far rear. Besides, small copies of the poster were printed on postal envelopes and postcards).

«Русские долго запрягают, да быстро едут» (russkie dolgo zapriagaiut da bystro edut) = an old figurative Russian proverb meaning "Russians get ready slowly but advance rapidly." Literally **запрягают** means [they] *harness.*

Сталинские соколы (stalinskie sokoly) = a wartime cliché for Soviet military airmen. Literally **Сталинские соколы** means "Stalin's falcons."

Чем ты сегодня помог фронту? (chem ty segodnia pomog frontu) = What have you done today to help the front? (Thousands of such posters were exhibited in every plant or factory in the Soviet far rear).

Что русскому здорово, то немцу смерть (chto russkomu zdorovo to nemtsu smert') = an old figurative Russian proverb, which states that Russians are much fitter for hard external conditions than other people, particularly the Germans. The word **здорово** in this context means *healthy.* Literally, then, the expression states, "What's healthy for the Russian is death to the German."

Several aphorisms and pithy expressions attributed to Field-Marshal A.V. Suvorov (repeatedly published in the Soviet wartime press)

Дисциплина – мать победы (distsiplina – mat' pobedy) = Discipline is victory's mother.

Каждый воин должен понимать свой манёвр (kazhdyi voin dolzhen ponimat' svoi maniovr) = Each warrior should understand his maneuver.

Кто удивил, тот победил (kto udivil tot pobedil) = The one who surprised [the enemy], that was the victor.

Легко в учении – тяжело в походе, тяжело в учении – легко в походе (legko v uchenii – tiazhelo v pokhode ...) = Easy in training – difficult in a campaign, difficult in training – easy in a campaign.

Пуля – дура, штык – молодец (pulia – dura, shtyk – molodets) = The bullet is a fool, [and] the bayonet is a dashing fellow.

Путь к сердцу солдата лежит через его желудок (put' k serdtsu soldata lezhit cherez ego zheludok) = The path to the soldier's heart lies through his stomach.

Сам погибай, а товарища выручай (sam pogibai a tovarishcha vyruchai) = Although you might be killed, you must rescue your comrade first.

Скорость нужна, а поспешность вредна (skorost' nuzhna a pospeshnost' vredna) = Speed is necessary, but haste is harmful.

13

Demotic Words and Phrases

Demotic Words & Phrases Related to a Person's Features

Баба (baba) [1] = a colloquial name for a woman. Sometimes it could be used with a trace of disrespect. However, in the "rural dialect" **баба** could also mean a wife.

«Баба» [2] and **слюнтяй** (sliuntiai) = two nicknames for a timorous, feeble, weak-willed man.

Бабёнка (babionka) = a lively young woman.

Бабка (babka) = a colloquial name for a grandmother.

Бабник (babnik) = a womanizer.

Балаболка (balabolka), **болтун** (boltun), **говорун** (govorun) and [a rude word] **мудозвон** (mudozvon) = a talkative person, a chatterbox.

Балда (balda), **болван** (bolvan), **дурак** (durak), **идиот** (idiot), **лопух** (lopukh), **придурок** (pridurok), **тупица** (tupitsa), and **тупоголовый** (tupogolovyi) = terms for a stupid person, a fool or a blockhead. Literally **лопух** is the Russian name for *burdock*.

Барыга (baryga), **барышник** (baryshnik), **перекупщик** (perekupshchik), and **спекулянт** (spekuliant) = contemptuous nicknames for a speculator who profits by purchasing goods at a low price and reselling them at a higher price.

Блатной (blatnoi) = a rogue, an illicit person, a criminal.

Брехун (brekhun), **враль** (vral') and **врун** (vrun) = a liar.

Бузотёр (buzotior) and **скандалист** (skandalist) = a person who creates scandals, a trouble-maker.

Вертихвостка (vertikhvostka) = a flirtatious woman.

Ворчун (vorchun) = a grumbler.

Гад (gad), **сука** (suka), **гнида** (gnida) and **ублюдок** (ubliudok) = slang terms for a harmful, odious, mean, obnoxious person. Literally **гад** means *a crawling reptile such as a snake*; **сука** means *a bitch*; **гнида** means *an egg or young form of a louse*.

Гнусавый (gnusavyi) and **гундосый** (gundosyi) = a person who speaks with an unpleasant nasal tone.

Горластый (gorlastyi) = a loud-mouthed go-getter.

«Делопут» (deloput) = a nickname for a man who mixes up anything he is dealing with.

«Дешёвка» (deshiovka) [1] = a nickname for a person or thing of no importance (also may relate to a shallow person).

«Дешёвка» [2] = a nickname for an available loose woman.

Дурнушка (durnushka) = an unattractive young woman; a plain Jane.

Жмот (zhmot) = a miser, a skinflint.

Заика (zaika) = a stutterer.

Замухрышка (zamukhryshka) = a homely, untidy person.

Зануда (zanuda) = a tiresome person, a pest.

Зараза (zaraza) = a slang term for a harmful, odious, mean, obnoxious person. Literally **зараза** means *an infection*.

«Звонарь» (zvonar') = a colloquial nickname for a person who is crazy about spreading any news all over. Literally **звонарь** means *a church bell ringer*.

Картавый (kartavyi) = a person who pronounces *r* with a burr.

Косноязычный (kosnoiazychnyi) = a person who speaks inarticulately.

Кривой (krivoi) = a person who is blind in one eye.

Крохобор (krokhobor) = a stingy hoarder.

Пацан (patsan) = a slang term for a boy.

Разгильдяй (razgil'diay), **нерадивый человек** (neradivyi chelovek), **расхлябанный человек** (raskhliabannyi chelovek) and **растяпа** (rastiapa) = terms for a lax, negligent person.

«**Размазня**» (razmaznia) = a nickname for a slack, hesitating person. Literally **размазня** means *a watery kasha*.

Робкий (robkii) = a timid person.

Рябой (riaboi) = a person whose face is pockmarked.

Сердцеед (serdtseied) = a man who is extremely attractive to women. Literally **сердцеед** means *a heart eater*.

Сиплый (siplyi) and **хриплый** (khriplyi) = a person who speaks hoarsely.

Сопляк (sopliak) = a scornful figurative name for an immature person. Literally **сопляк** is a nickname for *a snotty boy*.

Старый хрен (staryi khren) = an insulting colloquial nickname for an old man.

Тихоня (tikhonia) = a meek person.

Трепач (trepach) = a talkative gossip and fibber.

Хлюпик (khliupik) = a scornful colloquial term for a physically weak or weak-willed person.

Храпун (khrapun) = a snorer.

Шепелявый (shepeliavyi) = a lisper (a person who pronounces s like th in thick).

Шибздик (shibzdik) = a scornful colloquial term for a disrespected worthless person.

Языкастый (iazykastyi) and **языкатый** (iazykatyi) = a sharp-tongued person.

Other Demotic Words & Phrases

Барахлить (barakhlit') = to work unstably or in a seesaw manner like a roughly running engine.

Барахло (barakhlo) = secondhand odds and ends.

Батя (batia) = a colloquial friendly term for father. It is often used for some friend who is older than the speaking person. You could also hear **батя** among frontline soldiers when they referred to their wise, careful and kindhearted commander.

Бахнуть (bakhnut') and **бабахнуть** (babakhnut') = to thunder.

Белиберда (beliberda) = balderdash, senseless talk or writing.

Братцы (bratsy) = a colloquial friendly term for brothers, friends etc. It was mainly used in requests for help. So, a person, who suddenly became helpless, cries to people around him: **Братцы**, *help me!*

Быдло (bydlo) = a scornful term for a group of subordinate people (as a military detachment or unit) who performed any hard or dangerous job resignedly and without protest. During the war, especially in 1941-1942, many high Red Army commanders treated their subordinate troops as some **быдло**. Time and again Soviet soldiers and officers were unwisely sent to face certain death.

«Взять» (vziat') and **«забрать»** (zabrat') = figurative colloquial verbs that meant to arrest, to take into custody. These words were in widespread use in the pre-war years when Stalin's rule had jailed hundreds of thousands of innocent Soviet people. Literally **взять** means *to take* and **забрать** means *to take away*.

«Взять на пушку» (vziat' na pushku) and **«купить»** (kupit') = figurative expressions meaning to bluff, to fool etc. Literally they mean *"to take on a cannon"* and *"to buy"* respectively.

Восвояси (vosvoiasi) = a Russian colloquial (and a little ironical) adverb, which originally meant backwards or in the direction of home. For example: *Our attack failed and we had no choice but to return* **восвояси**.

Вот-вот (vot-vot) = something just about to happen or appear.

Врассыпную (vrassypnuiu) = helter-skelter; every which way.

Врезать, вжарить, влупить, влепить (vrezat', vzharit', vlupit', vlepit') = Russian colloquival verbs that mean *to deliver a blow*.

Головомойка (golovomoika) = a reprimand.

Гробануть (grobanut') and **угробить** (ugrobit') = figurative verbs that mean to force somebody or something to end badly or tragically). Literally **гробануть** and **угробить** mean *to put something/somebody into a coffin*.

Давеча (davecha) = (*obsolete*) shortly before the present moment.

«Дело – табак» (delo tabak) and **«Дело – труба»** (delo truba) = colloquial expressions to signify that things look bad. Literally **дело** means *affair, business, action*; **табак** means *tobacco*; and **труба** means *a pipe*.

Дерьмо (der'mo) = a colloquial word that refers to anything of bad quality or to any bad person. It can be also used as a curse. Literally **дерьмо** means *shit*.

Дерьмо собачье (der'mo sobach'e) = dog shit.

Достать (dostat') = to exhaust somebody's patience. Literally **достать** means *to reach, to take, to touch something.*

Драить (drait') = to scrub, to shed luster on the scrubbed surface.

Дрейфить (dreifit') and **трусить** (trusit') = to be afraid, to fear.

«Забирать» (zabirat') = a figurative colloquial verb that means to arrest or to draft. Literally **«забирать»** can be translated as *to detract.*

«Забрить» (zabrit') = a figurative colloquial verb that means to draft. (**«забрить»** comes from **брить** which means *to shave.* The first operation that any recruit had to undergo in the Red Army was the so-called zero-haircut – a closely shaved head.

Завалить (zavalit'), **шлёпнуть** (shliopnut') and **кокнуть** (koknut') = figurative colloquial verbs that mean to kill a person or an animal. Literally **завалить** means *to tilt downward* and **шлёпнуть** means *to slap.*

«Загибать» (zagibat') and **«заливать»** = to exaggerate, to tell lies. Literally **загибать** means *to bend something* and **заливать** means *to flood something.*

«Зажимать» (zazhimat') = to refuse to share something with others. Literally **зажимать** means *to squeeze, clench, bind, or clutch together.*

Зазноба (zaznoba) = a sweetheart.

«Заткнись!» (zatknis') = "Shut up!" or "Stuff it!" Literally **заткнись** means *cork yourself.*

Зенки (zenki) = an insulting colloquial word for eyes. **Заливать зенки** (zalivat' zenki) is a figurative phrase for *to drink alcohol excessively.*

Зуб на зуб не попадает (zub na zub ne popadaet) = a figurative colloquial expression that describes a person's teeth chattering.

«Каша» (kasha) = a mishmash, a mess. Literally **каша** means *boiled buckwheat groats.*

Кемарить (kemarit') = a Russian colloquial verb meaning *to nap.*

Копаться (kopat'sia) and **ковыряться** (kovyriat'sia) = to work unskillfully or clumsily at something.

Кулички (kulichki) [as in **это было где-то у чёрта на куличках** [eto bylo gde-to u chiorta na kulichkakh]) = it was somewhere very distant.

Ляп-тяп (liap-tiap) and **тяп-ляп** (tiap-liap)**; наспех** (naspekh) and **кое-как** (koe-kak) = to perform a work hurriedly, carelessly or haphazardly; a slapdash performance.

Мандраж (mandrazh) = a colloquial word for the state of being scared.

Навалиться (navalit'sia) = a figurative verb that means to attack heavily. Literally **навалиться** means *to lean one's weight upon something/somebody.*

Надавать, отделать, отлупить, дать дрозда, дать духу, дать прикурить (nadavat', otdelat', otlupit', dat' drozda, dat' dukhu, dat' prikurit') = Russian colloquial verbs that mean *to beat/punish strongly* (as enemy troops or a person).

Наломать дров (nalomat' drov) [1] = to have done something very stupid, to make a serious unintentional blunder.

Наломать дров [2] = to cause great damage intentionally (as to the enemy by a bombardment etc.) Literally **наломать дров** means *to break* [withered] *thin trees or branches for firewood.*

Намедни (namedni) = (*obsolete*) recently, a day or two ago.

На полную катушку (na polnuiu katushku) = a figurative expression that means completely/in a full measure. Literally **полная катушка** means *a full spool.*

Нары (nary) and **двухъярусные нары** (dvukh'iarusnye nary) = plank beds and bunk plank beds respectively.

«На халяву» (na khaliavu) = getting something for free.

«Несолоно хлебавши» (nesolono khlebavshi) = an old Russian figurative expression which describes that someone stopped his/her effort after seeing that it's failing or stopped waiting for some positive result after seeing his/her expectation dashed. For example: "That night our squad's mission was to capture a prisoner for interrogation. Unfortunately, the enemy launched illuminating flares all night long and we returned **несолоно хлебавши.**" Literally **«несолоно хлебавши»** could be translated as *"after eating an unsalted meal."*

Нынче (nynche) [1] = (*obsolete*) today.

Нынче [2] = a figurative term for at present.

Оплошать (oploshat') and **обмишулиться** (obmishulit'sia) = to make a foolish or stupid mistake; to screw up.

Отсидеть (otsidet') = a figurative colloquial verb that means to complete serving one's sentence.

Пайка (paika) = a colloquial term for an allotted portion of rationed food, usually a daily quota of bread (**пайка хлеба** [paika khleba]). During the war the quota was very small in the far rear, about 400 grams for a student or for a retired person.

Пахать (pakhat') = a figurative verb that means to perform a stint of long hard work. Literally **пахать** means *to plow.*

Пацанва (patsanva) = slang term for a group of boys collectively, boyhood.

По блату (po blatu) = obtained through good connections.

Подельники (podel'niki) = partners in crime; accomplices; henchmen.

Подмахнуть (podmakhnut') = to sign [a document] negligently or illegibly.

«Поехали!» (poiekhali) = "Let's go!" (An exclamation for starting some action etc. **«Поехали!»** is also a popular toast). Literally **поехали** means *have driven off.*

Полуторка (polutorka) = a colloquial name for a Soviet truck that has a 1.5 metric ton carrying capacity.

Получить взбучку [нагоняй, нахлобучку] (poluchit' vzbuchku [nagoniai, nakhlobuchku]) = to be hauled or raked over the coals.

Получить срок (poluchit' srok) and **схлопотать срок** (skhlopotat' srok) = to receive a prison sentence of some years.

«Помалкивай!» (pomalkivai) = "Keep silent!" or "Hold your tongue!"

«Посадить» (posadit') = to jail. Literally **посадить** means *to plant as a seed* and *to offer a seat.*

«Приказал долго жить» (prikazal dolgo zhit') and **«сыграл в ящик»** (sygral v iashchik) = two figurative ironic expressions meaning someone has died. Literally **приказал долго жить** means [someone] *has been ordered to live for a long time*; **сыграл в ящик** means [someone] *has played into a box.*

Примоститься (primostit'sia) = to find room in an uncomfortable place, as on the very edge of an occupied bed.

«Проталкивать» (protalkivat') = to nudge; to lobby.

«Пустить в расход» (pustit' v raskhod) = *(WW I)* a figurative expression that means to kill, to annihilate, to finish off. Literally **расход** means *expenses.*

«Пшик» (pshik) = a colloquial expression for the emptiness or nothing which has resulted from an unsuccessful attempt.

Пырнуть (pyrnut') = a colloquial verb which means to deliver a thrust as with a bayonet or with the point of a knife.

Раскиснуть (raskisnut') [1] = to lose firmness, force, energy, etc., as of character.

Раскиснуть [2] = to became soaked or saturated, as a dirt road.

Ржать (rzhat') = to laugh loudly. Literally **ржать** means *to neigh.*

Раздолбать (razdolbat') = to beat/smash (as the enemy) completely. Literally **раздолбать** means *to gouge completely.*

Сабантуй (sabantui) = a figurative name for any mass noisy event as a battle or a loud argument of several persons. Literally **сабантуй** means *Tatar fun festival.*

Сачковать (sachkovat') and **отлынивать** (otlynivat') = to goof off, to shirk one's work.

Сорваться (sorvat'sia) and **вспыхнуть** (vspykhnut') = to lose one's temper; to feel a fit of anger. Literally **сорваться** means *to break, to fall down, to dart off;* **вспыхнуть** means *to ignite, to flare up etc.*

«Сходить до ветру» (skhodit' do vetru) = to go to the toilet. Literally **сходить до ветру** means *to go to the wind* (because most toilets in the Russian countryside are situated outdoors).

Тары-бары (tary-bary), **болтовня** (boltovnia) and **пустые разговоры** (pustye razgovory) = a chit-chat, idle talks.

Тащить на горбу (tashchit' na gorbu) = to carry heavy items by oneself. Literally **тащить** means *to pull, to drag,* and **горб** means *a hump.*

«Тише едешь – дальше будешь» (tishe edesh dalshe budesh) = an old Russian folk wisdom which could be translated as "The slower you go – the farther you'll get" (This original wisdom had been modernized ironically: **«Тише едешь – дальше будешь от того места куда едешь»** [... ot togo mesta kuda edesh'] = "The slower you go – the farther you'll find yourself from your destination.")

Толкучка (tolkuchka) = a colloquial name for a crowded area where petty merchants and buyers unintentionally jostle each other. Literally **толкучка** is a colloquial term for *a shoulder to shoulder gathering.*

Травить (travit') [1], **трепаться** (trepat'sia) and **трепать языком** (trepat' iazykom) = to tell fanciful stories, to twaddle.

Травить [2] = to poison.

Травить [3] = to slip (as an anchor chain or a mooring rope).

Тьма (t'ma) [1], **мрак** (mrak), **темень** (temen') and **темнота** (temnota) = darkness, gloom.

Тьма [2] = a great many; scores of something.

Тьма тьмущая (t'ma t'mushchaia) = an innumerable amount of items or creatures.

Тянуть волынку (tianut' volynku), **волынить** (volynit'), **разводить бодягу** (razvodit' bodiagu) and **тянуть резину** (tianut' rezinu) = to act too slowly (very often – intentionally so); to drag one's feet.

«Уматывай!», «Убирайся отсюда!», «Уйди с глаз!», «Топай отсюда!», «Пошёл подальше!» (umatyvai, ubiraisia otsiuda, uidi s glaz, topai otsiuda, poshiol podal'she) = slang expressions for *Disappear!*, *Scram!* or *Get out of here!*

Устроить баню (ustroit' baniu) = to arrange a bloody defeat of the enemy. Literally **устроить баню** means *to arrange a washing such as in a bathhouse.*

Утка (utka) = a bedpan. Literally **утка** means *a duck.*

Филькина грамота (fil'kina gramota) = a demotic description of an invalid/wrongly composed/illegibly or untidily written/illiterate document.

«Хана» (khana), **«капут»** (kaput), **«кранты»** (kranty), **«труба»** (truba) = slang terms for an extremely unhappy, sometimes fatal ending.

Химичить (khimichit') = to use cunning, to trick.

Хлеб – всему голова (khleb vsemu golova) = bread is the master of all. Literally: *bread is the head of anything.*

Хреновина (khrenovina) = a colloquial word for something difficult to name, describe or explain.

Хреновый (khrenovyi) = bad.

Чепуха (chepukha) [1], **мелочь** (meloch'), **пустяк** (pustiak) and **ерунда** (erunda) = a trifle, a phenomenon or a creature of a little significance.

Чепуха [2] = meaningless words or ideas.

Что надо (chto nado) = of highest quality. Literally – *it's what you need.*

Шашни (shashni) = love affairs.

Швабра (shvabra) = a swab.

Швабрить палубу (shvabrit' palubu) = to swab a/the deck.

Шкандыбать (shkandybat') = slang term that means to limp.

Шуровать (shurovat') = a colloquial verb: to search secretly through somebody's belongings for the purpose of stealing something. Literally **шуровать** means *to stir up (a fire) as with a poker.*

Indecent and Vulgar Words, Phrases and Expressions

Блядь (bliad') [1], **курва** (kurva), **потаскуха** (potaskukha), **проститутка** (prostitutka) and **шлюха** (shliukha) = a whore, a prostitute. These words could be also used as a curse and, in this sense, might pertain either to a woman or to a man

Блядь [2] = Some crude people of low education, while narrating a story or speaking in a conversation, repeatedly used **блядь** as a word that carries no real meaning (equally with such English words as OK, well, so, you know). Some such "speakers" replace **блядь** with **блин** (blin) to keep their speech decent. Literally **блин** means *a pancake.*

Давать (davat') = (of a woman) to give – to have sexual intercourse with a man willingly

Дрочить (drochit') = a slang Ukrainian verb meaning *to masturbate, to frig.*

Мудак (mudak) = an indecent and at the same time a more contemptuous nickname for a fool.

Не пугай девку мудями (ne pugai devku mudiami) = don't frighten an experienced person with some of his/her habits. Literally: *Don't frighten a whore with your testicles*

Овладеть (ovladet') = (of a man) to take – to have a sexual intercourse with a woman Literally **овладеть** means *to take possession of something.*

Отдаваться (otdavat'sia) = (of a woman) to give oneself – to yield sexually.

Отлить (otlit') – an indecent verb for **писать** (pisat') and **мочиться** (mochit'sia) = to urinate. Literally **отлить** means *to pour off some available liquid.*

Пердун (perdun) = a rather rude colloquial name for a person, who farts loudly.

Поиметь (poimet') = (of a man) to have a sexual intercourse with a woman; to fuck a woman.

Скурвиться (skurvit'sia) = to become a total bastard (see **курва** above).

«Слаба на передок» (slaba na peredok) = an expression that describes a woman, who continually strives for sexual contact. (Other meanings of **передок** see in Chapter 15).

«Справлять большую нужду» (spravliat' bol'shuiu nuzhdu) = a half-indecent expression meaning to defecate. Literally, to deal with a larger need.

«Справлять малую нужду» (spravliat' maluiu nuzhdu) = a half-indecent meaning to urinate. Literally, to deal with a lesser need.

Хрен (khren) = a substitute for a Russian curse word that means penis. Literally **хрен** means *a horseradish*.

Целка (tselka) = a slang term for a virgin. (The adjective **целый** means *intact*).

14

Exclamations, Imperatives, Emotional Calls, Phrases etc.

Аврал! (avral) = (nautical, naval) All hands on deck!

Ага. = expresses confirmation or compliance with what was said to the speaker just now
It could be translated into English as yes, yep, OK.

Ага, and **Ага!** = express malicious joy.

Баста! (basta) = No more of this!/Enough!

Была не была (byla ne byla) = an interjectional expression that someone expresse
aloud or to oneself while making a difficult decision, especially about undertaking
a risky action.

Воздух! (vozdukh) = an alert shout notifying an air raid.

Вот тебе (и) на (vot tebe [i] na), also **вот те на (vot te na) and вот те раз (vot te
raz)** = expressions indicating a speaker's surprise or bewilderment.

Вот это да! (vot eto da) = expresses surprise along with positive emotions because o
what the speaker had just seen, heard or got to know.

Есть! (est') and its slangy version **Бу[дет] сделано!** (bu[det] zdelano) = a subordinate'
affirmative reply to a commander's order. Literally «**Бу[дет] сделано!**» means *"[It
will be done!"*

Зараза! (zaraza) = expresses a strong irritation, specifically because of an unsuccessfu
attempt. (See also **Зараза** in Chapter 13).

Караул! (karaul) = a shout for immediate help.

Ну и ну! (nu i nu) = an expression of surprise.

Ого! (ogo) = an expression of speaker's astonishment regarding something enormous o
extremely rare. **Ого-го!** (ogo-go) = an emphasized form of **Ого!**

Отбой! (otboi) [1] = the final call of the day. It sounds after the bedtime roll call.

Отбой! (otboi) [2] = the all-clear signal that cancels an air-raid warning .

Отставить! (otstavit') = Cancel!

Ох! (okh) = Ouch!, Oh!

Подъём! (podiom) = Reveille! – a signal to wake up.

Полундра! (polundra) = an alert signifying danger on or near the ship. It requires all hands to be on deck immediately. When the Soviet marines fought on land as common infantrymen, their war cry was **Полундра!** instead of "Hurrah!"

Стой! (stoi) and **Стоять!** (stoiat') = Stop!

Стой, кто идёт? (stoi kto idiot) = Stop, who goes there?

Стоять на месте! (stoiat' na meste) = Stand still! Freeze!

Стой, стрелять буду! (stoi streliat' budu) = Stop or I'll shoot!

Угу (ugu) = expresses confirmation or compliance with what was said to the speaker just now. **Угу** could be translated into English as *yes, yep, OK.*

Ура (ura) = expresses moderate joy or just satisfaction regarding to a recent result.

Ура! = a war cry that preceded or accompanied an attack. (In everyday life **Ура!** expresses wild joy)

Ух какой (ukh kakoi) = strengthens the expressiveness of following word(s). **For example: «Он был ух какой загорелый».** (on byl ukh kakoi zagorelyi) means *"He was extremely sunburned."*

Ух ты! (ukh ty and ukh ty) = expresses surprise.

Фу! (fu) = can express either a rebuke or an annoyance or disgust (resembles the old English expressions "Fee!" or "Fi!").

Фу-ты (fu-ty) = can express either surprise or irritation.

Фу-ты ну-ты (fu-ty nu-ty) = can express either surprise or irony.

Шабаш! (shabash) = Stop working!

«Шухер!» (shukher) = a slangy exclamation of an alarm.

Эй! (ei) = a shout used to attract somebody's attention.

Эх (ekh) = can express regret, reproach or anxiousness about something.

15

Frontline Slang, Phrases and Soldiers' Humor

«Автоматчики» (avtomatchiki) = a nickname for lice. The Russian word **автоматчики** literally means submachine gunners.

«Аллюр три креста» (alliur tri kresta) = at the double quick, at a breakneck speed.

«Бандеровцы» (banderovtsy) = colloquial names for members of Western Ukraine "Bandera guerillas" combat groups and detachments of Bandera's partisans which performed attacks and acts of terrorism against State and local authorities as well as against policemen and army detachments. Before September 1939, Western Ukraine was a part of Poland, then became a part of the USSR. In 1941-44, when Western Ukraine was occupied by Germany, "Bandera guerillas" forces temporarily acted as German military units. Stepan Bandera, the famous Ukrainian nationalist and anti-Communist, led his subordinates under the slogan "For Independent Ukraine!" Nowadays, his role is appraised in Ukraine extremely ambivalently.

«Бантик» (bantik) = a Russian nickname given to the Bantam Army Jeep BRC-40. These jeeps were a part of the American lend-lease program of assistance to the USSR. Literally **бантик** means *a small decorative knot.*

«Власовцы» (vlasovtsy) = a colloquial name for the personnel of the **РОА** (roa) Army. (**РОА** is the Russian abbreviation of **Российская Освободительная Армия** [rossiiskaia osvoboditel'naia armiia]) which means the *Russian Liberation Army.* The **РОА** Army was a German Wehrmacht formation consisted of over 100,000 men. Its commander was General **Власов** (Vlasov), the former Red Army Lieutenant-General, who had been taken prisoner in 1942. Soon after his capture, Vlasov proposed the German High Command to form an anti-Soviet army of former Soviet prisoners. **«Власовцы»** fought against the Red Army desperately. After the war Vlasov was captured by the Red Army troops and sentenced to death. A lot of former **«власовцы»** were shot or put into Soviet concentration camps after the war. This term was applied to any Soviet Slav serving with the *Wehrmacht,* whether or not they were actual ROA personnel.

«Бои местного значения» (boi mestnogo znacheniia) = a hackneyed expression used in the Soviet High Command's communiqùes when the Red Army troops were losing battles. Literally **бои местного значения** means *battles of local significance.*

«Драпать» (drapat') = to run without a backward glance, to skedaddle.

«Драп-марш» (drap-marsh) = a rout.

«Иконостас» (ikonostas) = a nickname for a collection of decorations on the frontline soldier's/officer's chest. (Also, see A special note in Chapter 9). Literally **иконостас** means *a wall in an orthodox church on which icons are placed, separating the sanctuary from the main part of the church.*

«Как штык» (kak shtyk) = a funny expression that describes someone's perfect state or his readiness to do something. For example: when a soldier was asked whether he is ready to go for a "tongue" (see **язык** below), his cheerful reply was **«Как штык!»** Literally **как штык** means *like a bayonet.*

«Кобра» (kobra) = a nickname for the American fighter Bell P-39 Airacobra. Over 4,500 of these fighters were shipped to the USSR according to the lend-lease program. Literally **кобра** means *cobra.*

«Краснопузая козявка» (krasnopuzaia koziavka) = a scornful nickname for infantrymen collectively and for the infantry as a whole. **Краснопузая козявка** could be translated as *red-bellied pipsqueak.*

«Кукушка» (kukushka) = a nickname for the Finnish snipers who often took their position among the branches of a tree. Literally **кукушка** means *a cuckoo bird.*

«Матильда» (matil'da) = a Russian colloquial name for the British A12 Matilda Mk II tank. It was suitable only for good roads, which were rare in the USSR. Thus, these tanks were breaking down all the time. Therefore the Red Army tank crew members nicknamed this tank **«капризная бабёнка»** (kapriznaia babionka) which means *"a capricious young woman."*

«Махнём не глядя!» (makhniom ne gliadia) = a very popular invitation among Red Army soldiers for a joyful speculative swap, where both participants don't know what small thing the other is hiding in his fist. These exchanges took place in Germany at the very end of the war and during initial postwar weeks. Usually the hidden things were watches taken from Germans, both captive soldiers and common civilians. As a rule, these watches were cheap because of their poor quality and Red Army soldiers nicknamed them **«штамповка»** (see Chapter 12).

Немец (nemets) = a German. At the same time, in a colloquial speech **немец** could mean a great number of Germans.

Немецкая подстилка (nemetskaia podstilka) = a woman on occupied territory, who slept with Germans. Literally **подстилка** means *a bottom layer* (such as a welcome mat, bed sheet or tablecloth etc.)

Немчура (nemchura) = a colloquial plural of **немец**. Usually **немчура** expresses a scornful attitude toward Germans.

«ОБС» (obees) – = abbreviated **одна баба сказала** (odna baba skazala) – defines the information at hand as a rumor. Literally **одна баба сказала** means: *one woman said...* (In Russian pronunciation **«ОБС»** sounds somewhat similar to **ОВС** (see Chapter 11)

«Освобожденец» (osvobozhdenets) = a "liberated man," who had been residing in Soviet territory that had just been liberated from German occupation and who had just been called up to the Red Army. Often they were sent to the front line still clothed in their everyday dress. Therefore another nickname for them was **«чернорубашечники»** (chernorubashechniki) which means *"those who wear black shirts"*. In 1943-44 the majority of the "liberated men" were from the Ukraine. There were among them also those who once had deserted from the Red Army and had settled comfortably in the occupied territory for some two years. In general, the "liberated men" were treated circumspectly in their new units, at least initially. **«Вояка 5-го Украинского фронта»** (voiaka piatogo Ukrainskogo Fronta) = "a warrior of the 5th Ukrainian Front" was a scornful nickname for a "liberated man" because only four Ukrainian Fronts actually existed and the fifth one implies his long peaceful and comfortable life while millions of Red Army soldiers continued taking part in bloody combats.

Отстреляться (otstreliat'sia) = a colloquial verb used to express informally that an artillery detachment/artilleryman completed its/his fire mission. For example, a gun platoon commander, after the platoon completed shooting at an appointed target, informally reports to the battery commander: **«Мы отстрелялись»** (my otstrelialis'). **Отстреляться** was often similarly used everywhere in everyday life.

«Парни, мы голодны – пора открыть второй фронт» = "Guys, we are hungry – it's time to open a 'Second Front' immediately" (a mocking suggestion to open an American tin can of Spam, which was a part of the lend-lease program of assistance to the USSR). Note: Opening a second front was a Soviet reference to the long-desired Allied invasion of Northern Europe. Initially it was planned to begin in 1942. Actually it started on D-Day in 1944.

«Передок» (peredok) [1] = a colloquial shortened form of a noun **передовая** (peredovaia) that means *a forward line of an acting troop's position*.

Передок [2] = a limber as for towing a gun.

«Покупатель» (pokupatel') = a colloquial figurative name for an official who recruits and enlists personnel for military service with a certain unit or detachment. Literally **покупатель** means *a buyer*.

«ППЖ» (pepezhe) – a Russian abbreviation for **полевая походная жена** (polevaia pokhodnaia zhena) = a "campaign wife", who cohabited usually with an officer of any marital status, mainly in the hope of becoming his legal wife. Almost any Red Army woman in a unit was looked upon by the male officers as a potential **ППЖ.**

Literally **полевая походная жена** means *a field marching wife*. This was a play on the similarly sounding PPSh, the submachine gun.

«Прощай, родина!» (proshchai rodina) = a nickname for both the Soviet 45mm anti-tank gun and the Soviet 76mm regimental field gun. The same nickname had been applied to the crews of both mentioned models of guns. Literally **«Прощай, родина!»** means *"Farewell motherland!"*

«Самоварщик» (samovarshchik) = a nickname for a mortar man.

«Славяне» (slaviane) and **«Братья славяне»** (brat'ia slaviane) = "Slavs" and "Brothers Slavs" – a friendly hello to a group of front-line soldiers. For example: "Hey, Slavs! What is the best way to the regimental HQ?" It didn't matter who these soldiers were – Russians, Ukrainians or Tatars, Uzbeks, Armenians etc.

Смазать (smazat') and **промазать** (promazat') – two colloquial forms of **промахнуться** (promakhnut'sia) = to fail to hit a target. Literally both **смазать** and **промазать** mean *to smear*.

Стрелять в белый свет, как в копейку (streliat' v belyi svet kak v kopeiku) = a figurative expression which means to shoot at random or by guess-work. A literal translation of the expression is: *to shoot at the whole wide world like at a kopek.*

Стрелять по своим (streliat' po svoim) = to shoot at one's own forces' positions, to commit a friendly fire incident..

Сухой паёк (sukhoi paiok) = dry ration – dried slices of bread, canned meat, some salt and sugar etc.

«Тотальная мобилизация» (total'naia mobilizatsiia) = a figurative term for an initial way to replenish the ranks of battered frontline rifle unit by transferring soldiers from the rear and auxiliary detachments into it. Literally **тотальная мобилизация** means *total mobilization.*

«Трепак» (trepak) = a soldiers' jargon name for the venereal disease gonorrhea (also known in Russia as **триппер** [tripper]). Literally **трепак** is the name of an old-fashioned Russian folk dance.

Фрицы (fritsy) = a colloquial plural of **Фриц** (frits) which was a slang, sometimes offensive, for a German, especially for a German soldier. Literally **Фриц** is the German male first name Fritz spelled in Russian.

«Язык» (iazyk) = a prisoner captured for interrogation. Literally **язык** means *a tongue* or *language.*

Some special phrases

Soldiers from Central-Asian Soviet Republics were tea-lovers. They advised their Russian-speaking frontline friends: «**Пей чай – будешь сильным. Вода крепкая – пароходы держит**» = *"Drink tea – you will be strong. Water is strong – it holds ships."*

While experiencing "starvation rations," natives from Central-Asian Soviet Republics complained in a figurative manner: «**Товарищ лейтенант, курсак совсем пропал**» = *"Comrade Lieutenant, my kursak has disappeared completely"* (kursak means *belly*).

An informal humorous reveille in Ukrainian: «**Хлопці, на висцик!**» (khloptsi na vystsyk) = *"Guys, get up and take a leak!"*

Examples of "encoding" some restricted information (as in telephone communications, etc.)

«**Карандаш**» (karandash) = a rifle. Literally **карандаш** means *a pencil*.

«**Нитка**» (nitka) = a long wire used in field telephone systems. Literally **нитка** means *a thread*.

«**Огурцы**» (ogurtsy) = shells. Literally **огурцы** means *cucumbers*.

«**Семечки**» (semechki) = rifle cartridges. Literally **семечки** means *sunflower seeds*.

«**Ствол**» (stvol) = a barrel. The term was mostly used as a unit of artillery strength. For example, a regiment commander reported to a divisional staff: *"All my «***стволы***» are ready to begin the bombardment."*

«**Хозяин**» (khoziain) = a unit's commander. Literally **хозяин** means *a master, a boss, a landlord*.

«**Штык**» (shtyk) and «**активный штык**» (aktivnyi shtyk) = a rifleman fit for fighting. Literally **штык** means *a bayonet* and **активный штык** means *an active bayonet*.

An example of a road sign: «**Хозяйство Иванова —> »** = "Ivanov's household —>" – pointed the direction to the unit, the commander of which was named Ivanov.

A few funny anecdotes and amusing soldiers' tales which were popular at the front

Half-forgotten funny anecdotes of the old Russia

Sometimes Husbands' Smoking Does their Wives Good

A middle-aged woman and her twenty-something-old married daughter strolled along the main street of a town. In front of a tobacco store the woman addressed her daughter:

- Please wait for me for a short while. I need to glance at something inside...

The daughter seemed surprised:

- Mom, as I know, Dad stopped smoking six months ago while you're a permanent non-smoker...

The mother (blushing shyly):

- Don't you know, we discovered that after resuming smoking he performs his matrimonial duties more effectively. Now he needs three cartons of cigarettes per month.

The daughter (blushing shyly, too):

- Oh Mom, I'd like to buy some cigarettes for my husband, too. Let's enter the store together!

A Lucky Pavement Sweeper

Early in the morning a middle-aged man was sweeping the pavement in front of his master's house. While performing each sweep of the broom to his right, the man said: *"This way is good."* As he swept to the left, the man would say: *"This way is good, too."*

An elderly master's gardener quietly stepped up to the sweeper and asked: *"What do your phrases really mean?"*

The sweeper revealed: *"Last night was a success for my family. First, I had sexual intercourse with my mistress and she repaid the pleasure with several bucks. That is the reason for 'This way is good.' Second, at the same time my master had sexual intercourse with my wife and he repaid the pleasure with several bucks. That is the reason for 'This way is good, too.'"*

A Naive Victim

A middle-aged woman brought a law suit against a man who had stolen her precious necklace. When the hearing of the case started, the judge asked her:

- Where was your necklace at the moment of the theft?

- It was on my neck, your Honor.

- Did you resist, as his hand reached for your neck?

- I offered no resistance to him, your Honor.

- Why?

- I thought that he was doing so with noble intentions, your Honor.

An Extremely Earnest Orderly

An HQ officer rented an apartment in St. Petersburg. His loyal orderly, Ivan by name, occupied a small room there. One Sunday the officer decided to reward the orderly for his diligence. Before noon the officer gave Ivan a leave-pass and one rouble in addition. The officer's parting words were:

- *Ivan, I recommend that you spend this ruble on a whore: just go to Ligovka Avenue and you'll see a lot of them. Choose the best to your liking. My only warning: your chosen one should be* **здоровая*** (zdorovaia) *because the gonorrhea disease is very likely among them.*

Ivan returned home at late afternoon. He thanked the officer with a low bow, while Ivan's smile expressed his full satisfaction. The officer's question, however, was absolutely serious:

- *Are you sure she was* **здоровая***?*
- *Surely! I could barely wrestle my ruble away from her!*

*The Russian adjective **здоровая** has two meanings: first – <u>healthy</u>; second – (colloquial) <u>strong</u>.

Some amusing anecdotes from WW II

Just Homonyms

It is late July of 1944. In a far rear Soviet city of N. two "white card" holders bumped into each other.

The first : *"Did you hear the latest Sovinformbureu's communique? Red Army troops have taken L'vov*!"*

The other: *"Let them take tigers also as long as the second category reserve remain untouched."*

*In Russian the name of the city of **L'vov** and accusative case of the word **lions** are 100% homonyms.

A Successful Trick

Several draftees were waiting for their turns near the entrance of the registration and enlistment office of the city of N. A medical examination commission was working in the building. One of the draftees was already examined and had been determined being able for military service. Now he was waiting for his friend, who was still in the building.

Finally, the smiling friend went out and a short conversation took place.

- *What about you?*
- *They didn't take me.*
- *Why not?*
- *Do you see a fly on the wall over the front door?*

- Yes, I do.
- Well, I don't.

A Stout Red Army Soldier against a Strong Drink

Late spring 1945: during street fighting in a German town, a Russian soldier entered a small pharmacy holding his submachine gun at ready. The frightened mistress was horror-stricken, while the soldier, after realizing where he was, began asking her in body language to pour a glass of spirits for him. The trembling woman poured some clear liquid into a glass. The soldier emptied the glass in one breath, then grunted with pleasure, wiped his lips with a sleeve and ran to catch up with his comrades. In a short while the mistress discovered that she had accidentally given the soldier some acid instead of spirits. Horrified that she had killed a human being, the woman fainted...

A month passed. Germany capitulated, and there was no more fighting. Suddenly, a smiling Russian soldier entered the pharmacy and the mistress recognized him at first sight. Seeing the soldier alive she felt happy and relieved. The soldier asked for one more glass of spirits. While pouring the alcohol, she confessed her previous error when pouring him a drink. The soldier reassured her with a gesture and pointing at a small hole in his right boot, said to himself in Russian: "Now I know how this hole got here!"

A Popular Riddle

Q. What is the difference between a bomb and a frontline girl?
A. A bomb is stuffed in the rear then sent to the front. For a frontline girl, it's the other way around.

A Foul-mouthed Marine

Mid summer 1944: a battle-hardened Marine received a two weeks leave as a battle honor and returned to his small home village. The next day all the women and girls gathered in his parents' yard, where some moonshine and meager refreshments were prepared. Everybody knew the guy was a good guitarist and singer, and soon they began asking him to perform some popular frontline song. However the guy hesitated, appealing to the fact that the song he wanted to play was full of foul language.

- *No problem*, – said the guy's girlfriend "just replace each improper word with *"la la."*

So the marine began singing:
La-la la-la la-la la-la la-la-la,
La-la la-la ass *la-la-la-la.*
La-la fuck you *la-la la-la la-la,*
La-la la-la la-la shit *la-la la-la...*

The song stopped abruptly: everybody, including the performer, roared with laughter and tears blurred many eyes...

Note: At that time Soviet Marines were well-known for their profane everyday language.

Rhymed humorous and vulgar expressions and playful folk songs

Прицел ноль-пять – По своим опять! (pritsel nol' piat' po svoim opiat') = *Sight zero-five – Again at ours!*

This rhymed expression describes a friendly fire incident. Riflemen often used it at the front to tease artillerymen (mostly undeservedly).

Полюбила лейтенанта – носит синие штаны,

Оказалось толку мало: все продукты у старшины! (poliubila leitenanta nosit sinie shtany okazalos' tolku malo vse produkty u starshiny) =

I fell in love with a lieutenant who wears blue trousers, [but]
It turned out not to make much sense, you see,
Because over all the rations the sergeant major has the power!

Полюбила лейтенанта, а майор мне говорит:

"У меня ремень пошире и звезда ярчей горит" (poliubila leitenanta a maior mne govorit u menia remen' poshire i zvezda iarchei gorit) =

I fell in love with a lieutenant but the major is telling me:
"My belt is wider [than his] and my star [on my shoulder strap] shines brighter [than his starlet]."

Не страшно, что морда телячья,

Была бы ... горячая (ne strashno chto morda teliach'ia byla by ... goriachaia) =

May she have a calves' mug
As long as her ... is hot.

Хорошо тому живётся, кто с молочницей живёт:

Молочко он попивает и молочницу ... (khorosho tomu zhiviotsia kto s molochnitsei zhiviot molochko on popivaet I molochnitsu ...) =

A soldier billeted to a dairy-maid
Feels in seventh heaven:
In addition to drinking milk
He manages to ... the maid.

Акулина, Акулина,

Молись Богу за меня:

У меня растёт ...,

Акулина, для тебя! (Akulina Akulina molis' bogu za menia u menia rastiot ...
Akulina dlia tebia) =

Akulina. Akulina,
Pray to Heaven for me:
I have a growing ...,
Akulina, for you!

Milton Keynes UK
Ingram Content Group UK Ltd.
UKHW022334180823
427126UK00005B/168